LIVING
SERVICE

Praise for:
Living Service: The Journey of a Prosperous Coach

If you're looking for a quick-fix, seven-step formula or tactics to get clients for your coaching practice, you won't find it here. What you will find, however, is much more valuable—the insight that "service isn't an external strategy; it's an internal stance." As a coach, you cannot take your clients where you have never been yourself. Melissa offers a brutally honest and vulnerable account of her own journey of struggle, failure, success, failure, and ultimate success— not as arriving, but as an ongoing journey. This book offers great lessons for any coach who wants to serve clients in the most powerful way.

~ **Ron Wilder,** creator of CEO Jiu-Jitsu and author of *Clear Your Hidden Profit Blocker(s): How to Own Your Next Level of Performance So There's No Looking Back, Aligned Action: The Key to CEO Effectiveness* and *The 100 Watt War*

Melissa Ford's insightful journey on her path to prosperous coaching is a MUST READ for everyone in the world of coaching!

~ **Steve Chandler,** Author of *Time Warrior: How to defeat procrastination, people-pleasing, self-doubt, over-commitment, broken promises and chaos*

The journey shared here is as honest and real as it gets. *Living Service* is for coaches who want better business results, deeper friendships, more genuine and loving family relationships, and an all-around great life. Melissa's heartfelt stories in *Living Service* are beautifully illustrated with humor, candor and light-heartedness.

~ **Sherry Welsh,** leadership coach and author of *Slowing Down: Unexpected Ways to Thrive as a Female Leader*

Melissa Ford is a brilliant coach, and in *Living Service* she takes us through her personal experiences with humor and clarity so we can learn from her wisdom firsthand. I am a better, more relaxed, and compassionate coach because of this book. One of the best books I've ever read on coaching.

~ **Tina Quinn,** Life Leadership Consultant, coach, speaker and author of *Invisible Things: The Most Important Things in Life Are the Ones You Can't See*

Melissa is a teacher, a compassionate guide, and someone who will always stand behind you and champion you. This book is more than a "how-to"—using service to get something. It's a doorway to transforming your life and the lives of those you serve.

~ **Gary L Mahler,** Mahler International Coaching Inc. Life, Business, Relationships, Leadership

A raw, honest look at what it takes to go from beginner to master. Melissa reminds us that coaching and service are not about systems, strategies and schemes. They are about being human and discovering a deeper connection with yourself, others and the world.

~ **William Giruzzi,** coach and author of *A Life Worth Living*

Melissa inspires the reader to move toward mastery of the coaching profession.

~ **Kamin Samuel,** leadership coach and author of *Wealth Transformation Journal* and *Increase Your Abundance Starting Today!*

Service—true service—is the key to a prosperous coaching practice. However, while this word is often used in the world of coaching, it is rare to find a coach who truly understands what it means to live as service. In her wonderful new book, Mellissa Ford shows us just how to do this, and how to build a full practice from this place.

~ **David Schwendiman,** coach, King of the Unicorns and author of *Selling from the Top of the Ladder: The Ultimate Sales Playbook*

Refreshingly honest and vulnerable in her sharing, Melissa Ford shows how far from understanding—let alone living—service she was. Through a series of personal stories, she beautifully illustrates her journey to understanding service and reimagines what it means to truly work, live, and love from a service mindset.

~ **Arminda Lindsay,** coach and host of *The All Arminda Show* podcast

This insightful, funny and powerful book sharing Melissa's journey from struggling to prosperous coach is a demonstration of pure service to the reader, a true gift from her heart to yours.

~ **Lisa Giruzzi,** transformative coach, author of *31 Days to Transform Your Life* and *Bringing Out the Best in Your Employees*

If your goal is to make an impact in people's lives and be successful doing it . . . Melissa shares her story with refreshing grit, humor and honesty that offers inspiration to serve powerfully—at your highest level, no matter where you start."

~ **Lori Hanson,** The Success Whisperer, author of *The Stress Survival Kit for the Alpha Female*

LIVING SERVICE

THE JOURNEY OF A
PROSPEROUS COACH

MELISSA FORD

MAURICE BASSETT

Living Service: The Journey of a Prosperous Coach

Copyright © 2019 by Maurice Bassett

All rights reserved. No part of this book may be reproduced or copied in any form without written permission from the publisher.

Maurice Bassett
P.O. Box 839
Anna Maria, FL 34216

Contact the publisher:
MauriceBassett@gmail.com
www.MauriceBassett.com

Contact the author:
www.melissafordcoaching.com

Illustrations and cover design: David Michael Moore
Editing and interior layout: Chris Nelson

ISBN: 978-1-60025-076-7

Library of Congress Control Number: 2019948178

First Edition

~ To ~

Steve Chandler

For hanging in there
and waking me up
(repeatedly)!

Table of Contents

Foreword by Ankush Jain	xiii
Introduction	xvii

Part I: Awakening to Service

1.	Breaking Up Is Hard to Do	3
2.	Off to a Nervous Start	8
3.	Hidden Help	10
4.	One-Sentence Wakeup Call	13
5.	What the Hell Is Service?	18
6.	My Sneaky Social Self	22
7.	From Fake Pro to Legit	25
8.	Another Piece of the Professional Puzzle: No Downside	30
9.	The Year I Set My Hair on Fire	35
10.	The Heart of the Matter	38

Part II: Learning Service

11.	Learning to Learn	43
12.	Learning Aversion	48
13.	H.O.W.	53
14.	Got Courage?	56
15.	Where Had I Not Been HONEST?	61
16.	How to Be OPEN	65
17.	Willing to Be WILLING?	69
18.	Three Stages of Mastery	71
19.	The Stages of Service Mastery #1: Love Your Process	74
20.	The Detour	79

21. #2: Own Your Progress _____ 82
22. #3: You've Got This! _____ 86
23. The Service Game _____ 91
24. Playing Without Fear _____ 94
25. Game On! _____ 100

Part III: Practicing Service

26. Mastery Milestones _____ 111
27. Recovering _____ 114
28. Drop that "Coaching" Thing _____ 120
29. Money Commits _____ 126
30. No Niche Necessary _____ 132
31. Working Coach vs. Prosperous Coach _____ 135
32. Fee Creation vs. Fee Confusion _____ 140
33. It Isn't a YES _____ 144
34. Sisyphus System _____ 149
35. Slowing Down to Powerfully Serve _____ 156
36. The Service Equation _____ 161

Part IV: Living Service

37. Service Clarity _____ 167
38. Service Is Creative _____ 171
39. Stay on the Path _____ 175
40. Serving Loved Ones _____ 178
41. Serving Yourself _____ 181
42. Keep Upgrading Your Service _____ 183
43. Service Becomes Your Life _____ 188
44. You're Right Where You Need to Be _____ 190

Acknowledgments _____ 195
About the Author _____ 199

Foreword

by Ankush Jain

Melissa Ford is an outstanding coach with a thriving coaching practice. She has no shortage of clients wanting to work with her, and throughout *Living Service* you'll see why.

So why write this book?

It's certainly not designed to give her credibility or establish her as an authority in this field. She already has all that. Nor is it to inflate her ego. I've had the pleasure of growing my own coaching practice alongside her through Steve Chandler's coaching school, and Melissa is one of the most humble, honest and down-to-earth people I know.

What Melissa does in this book is share her personal, honest and incredibly valuable insights into her journey as a coach, from her early struggles through to her ongoing success on the path of service. Only Melissa could have written this book, but within it you will find the kind of wisdom and guidance that will help illuminate your own journey, whether you're just starting or are already established.

I've witnessed firsthand many of the stories Melissa shares here, and I admire her courage to "tell it as it is." There is no preplanned script or formula in this book; rather it is an expression of pure service, no-holds-barred. As I read it I found myself spontaneously writing "Wow!" in the margins. There are few coaches who have the courage to be so honest, raw and authentic in a book about coaching.

One of many highlights for me is Melissa's exploration of the "H.O.W." acronym, which stands for "Honest," "Open" and "Willing." Isn't that a great way to approach the process of making powerful transformations in your life? Elsewhere she talks about the concept of recovering from coaching conversations gone wrong and reigniting her relationship with her prospects. Her words, "I found that I could always recover. Always." ring true not only for growing a coaching practice but for life as well. These are poignant reminders for me and ones I'll no doubt be sharing with my own clients.

Living Service is a book I know I'll read again and again. In fact, I wish I had read it years ago when I was trying to figure out how to make money in this profession called "coaching." The insight, humor and practical wisdom on these pages offer something for all coaches. I'm so glad I've had the chance to read it, and now our entire profession will benefit from this book being out in the world.

When you are able to shift your inner awareness to how you can serve others, and when you make this the central focus of your life, you will then be in a position to know true miracles in your progress toward prosperity.

~ Wayne W. Dyer

Introduction

When I first decided to *go pro* and make my living as a coach I wish there had been a book that pulled back the curtains so I could see the nitty-gritty of what it takes to build a prosperous business through service.

I wish there had been an honest, simple book to encourage me, one that infused a little humor into the ups and downs of the journey and offered me new ideas along the way.

The ideal book would normalize my experiences so I could cut myself some slack when I felt doubt or frustration or discouragement. It would allow me to hold those times lightly, to know that no matter how I might feel in any particular instance, those darker moments were not reflective of my limited abilities or lack of potential. They were only signs of the insecure thinking that all coaches experience, get into perspective and then move beyond.

In short, when I'd started on my own journey to becoming a prosperous coach, I wish I'd had a book like this one.

Today I've reached a level in my coaching practice where I've created more income than I ever imagined possible in those early days. I select my clients, and I live a wonderful life enriched by my work.

Accomplishing this required a major shift in my approach.

Prior to discovering service, my business plan was simple: get better and better as a coach and then people would naturally hire me. My coaching improved, but it didn't create paying clients. Success (and feeling good about my efforts) seemed far out of reach since I had a limited view of prosperity. I really had only one metric: making money.

Over time, with service as my guide, my understanding of prosperity expanded to include not only the profitability of my business but also my ability to thrive as a person.

I've witnessed so many new coaches who are busy doing things to grow their businesses: branding, podcasting, blogging, increasing their social media followers, and more. One of my clients spent her first few years working on her business by creating a beautiful website, a memorable logo, and an impressive Instagram presence—but she never created paying clients. She got tangled up in the illusion that because she was busy, she was progressing.

I see other coaches who are caught up in a way of being to grow their businesses, believing that if they're just heart-centered enough then paying clients will organically appear. Loving people and helping them is essential, but without establishing a professional relationship with your prospects and clients, this kind of service can be confusing. Are you helping as a paid professional or a good friend?

The truth is you need both *doing* and *being* to grow your business. The doing is a skillset for creating clients. The being is an internal place to come from, one of love, caring, and connection. When you meld these two together you create the service path: your own unique version of service. You express this in a powerful coaching conversation that makes a difference in someone's life. From this, prospects see that coaching with you creates a positive payoff, and so it makes good sense for the two of you to work together.

This book is about that approach: the path of service, and how it unfolded for me. My hope is that this book will inspire and inform you, and encourage you to stay on the path of learning and growing in service.

That's how clients are created.

It's also how prosperous coaches are created.

The path of living service.

You can't skip your own evolution.

~ **Steve Chandler**

1

Breaking Up Is Hard to Do

If you're lucky, life will be a series of wake-up calls that you answer rather than ignore and let go to voicemail. For years, I had been doing the latter, unknowingly committed to other things "more important" than waking up and consciously creating my life.

Some of those other things were important, such as taking care of my family, helping my husband with his business, doing odd jobs here and there . . . But I spent a lot of mental energy and time protecting myself from any thoughts or experiences that might make me feel bad about myself for not growing a profitable coaching business. It was much easier for me to blame others for my lack of progress so that I wouldn't be seen (or see myself) as someone who didn't have it all together. In service to self-preservation, I had been dedicated to putting my dream on hold.

It turns out that I didn't need to safeguard myself

from life. I needed to start living it. So I started where it made sense on my journey as a professional coach, a place I'm not sure many coaches begin: I became a barista at Starbucks.

My husband had been running his own business for the past seven years, having left behind the corporate world of plentiful perks such as expense accounts, cars, trips, phones, pensions, 401 (k)s and, most critical of all, medical insurance. It didn't take long for me to see what I had never before appreciated. Medical insurance premiums for a small business owner are astronomical—and the coverage it affords is minimal. But I'd heard that Starbucks offered excellent medical insurance for part-time workers, allowing me to cover any injuries incurred by my football-playing son and any illnesses in our family while I ramped up my coaching business.

I worked the opening shift, leaving my house at 3:30 a.m. so I could get this grind (pun intended) out of the way and leave my afternoons free to develop workshops with Karen, my dear friend and business partner.

But things weren't going according to plan. Karen and I were never able to get our levels of commitment to growing our business—or our calendars—to match up. Neither of us knew how to move forward, and each of us was waiting for the other to pull things together.

I was going through the motions, but in truth I'd given up hope that anything would ever come of it. Our progress was in a holding pattern and I felt the heavy weight of futility crushing in on me.

I trudged through my daily routine at Starbucks, returning home by early afternoon feeling numb and depleted. At the three-and-a-half-year mark, when other health insurance options became available, I quit Starbucks. I'd done what I'd set out to do, but the experience had stripped me down to basics. I'd invested so much of my psychic energy numbing my mind to get through my days that "anesthetized" had become my default setting.

One afternoon, not long after quitting Starbucks, I stood outside in my front yard. It was spring, the season of rebirth, and I was barefoot on the fresh grass. I was in the exact same place in my coaching career as when I'd first started my barista gig—stuck—except now I was three-and-a-half years older. As I surveyed my neighborhood block, none of the budding trees or newly emerging flowers looked bright or beautiful. Everything looked dull, grey and flat—reflecting exactly how I felt inside.

"Is this it?" I quietly asked myself.

"This can't be it," was my next thought.

Without making a conscious decision, I turned

around, walked back into the house and called Karen. As her phone rang, I reflected on how many times I'd backed away from this imminent conversation, consumed by worry that if I broke off our partnership, Karen would never talk to me again. Now I felt deeply compelled to speak the words that needed to be said.

She answered, and I said without preamble, "I think we each need to work on our own."

The words I'd kept under lock and key were now out in the open.

"You can do workshops and groups in your area, and I'll do them in mine. We can still share our content."

Karen sounded confused. "What do you mean?"

I hurried up, sounding apologetic. "I mean, we both created the content. We can share it. But I just need to work on my own."

"Is this what you've been trying to tell me for a while?" Karen asked.

"Yes," I admitted.

I felt sick inside, barely aware of what I was saying. The only thing stronger than my fear and nausea was the clear and urgent conviction that this was a matter of life and death. *Mine.* I needed to stop waiting and start doing, beginning with this call.

Karen agreed to my request and quickly got off the phone.

I sat down, feeling stunned. Karen was my closest friend and ally, a person I'd grown with for the past dozen-plus years. I had just severed my most vital connection.

It would be another six months before she even spoke to me again.

2

Off to a Nervous Start

The greatest irony was that Karen and I had spent all these years practicing a coaching technique called "The Option Method" in which we would trade off "dialogues" to identify and grow beyond our limiting beliefs. Clear, honest communication was an essential element of this practice, yet I had been shoving down all my feelings of frustration and anger, too scared to admit to myself that I didn't think I could venture out on my own. On one level I was hoping she would somehow save me and make this business work, all the while knowing on a deeper level that she wouldn't or couldn't.

It was unthinkable to me that now, at this stage of my life, I had failed to make any inroads on my coaching business. Ending my business partnership and, inadvertently, my friendship with Karen was my last-ditch attempt to turn my life around and make it work.

I was going to build a coaching practice or die trying.

Once I could no longer use Karen as an excuse for my failure to move forward, my commitment began to change. Instead of waiting, I was willing to take action, to do something different. But I didn't know what or how, and I needed someone's help.

That someone was a coach named Steve Chandler.

3

Hidden Help

I was nervous during my first conversation with Steve, sitting cross-legged on my bed and talking as softly as possible, like a teenager sneaking a forbidden call. I was keeping it on the down-low because my husband would never approve of me seeking assistance. He was an entrepreneur from the School of Hard Knocks and had a master's degree from the Boot-Strap-Your-Way-To-Success Business School. He was old-school skeptical. The coaching profession hadn't been around very long, so it was difficult for anybody who had worked as hard at business success as my husband had to see any value in spending money on coaching. (By the way, he is now one of my greatest supporters.)

But I was also skeptical, and I too found it hard to spend money on coaching. And it took me some time to see that simply having a few coaching sessions doesn't deliver success in this profession. Becoming a prosperous coach has to be treated as an apprenticeship.

So I talked with Steve about everything from my failure as a coach to my broken friendship with Karen, my sense of hopelessness and helplessness and how I'd wasted my life. I complained about all the people who didn't support me and who made it hard for me to be successful.

Steve didn't touch any of that. He didn't interrupt or judge me. He didn't try to give me advice or have me see the error of my ways. He just listened.

At the end of my monologue he simply asked if I would like to talk again. I was hesitant, having no idea of what else I'd talk about, but I knew I had to keep moving. So I agreed.

During our second conversation, I asked Steve how we'd work together and what he would charge. I needed someone with business experience to guide me forward. He explained his basic coaching package. Having never worked with a coach before—ironic, huh? A coach without a coach—I asked for further clarification.

"So," I asked, "I have ten sessions, and they each last an hour?"

"Yes, that's right."

"Okay. And how often do we schedule them? Weekly, bi-weekly, monthly?"

"You can use them whenever you want. The only

requirement is that you use them before I'm dead."

"Really?" I forced a laugh.

"Yes."

Now I was even more uncertain; for one thing, how old was this guy anyway?

Desperate to have someone teach me the "how-to's" of client creation, I agreed.

I figured that with no specific time frame, I'd be able to maximize my investment by using those coaching sessions *only when necessary*—provided Steve didn't up and die on me.

4

One-Sentence Wakeup Call

I eked out those sessions over the course of the next eighteen months. Nothing much happened. Steve and I had some nice chats. My mood improved, but I still struggled to get clients.

In fact, I didn't have any clients, but that wasn't because of my coach. I would use my sessions asking "how-to" questions so I could feel less fearful and hopefully know what to do. Then, I'd try to implement my newfound courage and discoveries—only to default back into the habitual thinking that kept me stuck. Since I had never been coached before, I thought I was being frugal spacing out my sessions with my coach. Instead, I was delaying my progress. I just couldn't create any momentum only talking every couple of months.

That was almost ten years ago. Today, Steve is still my coach.

Much has changed since then, including two very

important things: I get Steve's humor and I now understand the crucial role I need to play in my own development. Back then I was a passive participant waiting for my coach to do something for me that would magically get me clients. I figured that if I worked with a master coach like Steve, progress would have to occur.

No wonder my results were limited!

But I hung in there, and so did Steve. As we came to the end of our ten-session package, he encouraged me to join his upcoming Coaching Prosperity School. I could be with a group of coaches learning how to enroll clients and supporting each other along the way.

I was hesitant. The idea of spending more money (and having to tell my husband, who had no idea what I was up to) made my stomach turn.

Why would I make another investment when the first one hadn't delivered the desired results: clients, prospects in the pipeline and money? Worse still, there was no guarantee that a second investment would move the needle either.

I told Steve I'd think about it.

I did. I thought a lot about why it wasn't a good idea. The school required a commitment of six months, with three live meetings at various locales across the U.S. So not only would I incur the cost of tuition, but there would also be the added expenses of flights, hotels, food and transportation. Steve was asking me to spend money when I wasn't even making any!

I put the offer out of my mind until a few weeks later, when I received an email from Steve. It was short, containing one simple question:

```
When are you going to stop
living like you're never going
to die?
```

I caught my breath.

I read the question again, letting the truth of it fill me up.

Holy Shit! I *was* living like there was no end to this game called life. I was sitting on the sidelines *waiting* for something to happen!

Waiting for Steve's coaching to change me.

Waiting for clients to magically appear.

Waiting for my husband to be more supportive and believe in me so that I could believe in myself.

Just like I had done with Karen: waiting for someone to save me, because deep down I was so afraid I couldn't do it myself.

Steve's question woke me up to a sense of urgency I had never before experienced.

I saw that even though I talked a big game about how I wanted to build a strong coaching practice, my actions spoke otherwise.

I emailed back immediately, "Yes. I'm in! When does it start?"

A few years ago, I reminded Steve about that email. I was curious.

"Why," I asked him, "did your school require such a big financial investment, including flying to three different locations for live, in-person weekends? Why not some other option that was more convenient and affordable?"

His answer: "I didn't want it to be easy for you, as if

all you needed to do was put on your slippers and robe and shuffle down the hallway to your home office to catch a webinar. If it was easy, you wouldn't have really shown up. You wouldn't have been invested. I wanted your commitment to be strong."

Actually, my commitment *had* been strong—but not to growing a coaching business. Sure, that's what I'd been telling myself I wanted to do, but what I had really been committed to was excuse-making, blaming others and believing that somehow my life would simply align with my desires without any further input from me.

But that's not how it works, and at last I was beginning to see this. All along life had been on the other end of the line, demanding I step up and step into a new level of commitment on my path.

I finally answered the call.

5

What the Hell Is Service?

The first thing I heard in Steve's coaching school was that prosperous coaches focus their actions and communication on service—not marketing, sales or promotion.

What?

I had no reference point for what they were talking about. Growing up, the unwritten motto in my family was, "Every man, woman and child for themselves." We were an independent group. Of course, we would help and support each other, but when it came to reaching out beyond our family unit and into our community, we just didn't do that. We didn't volunteer for things, and there was certainly no talk of "giving back."

Well into my adulthood, I did not understand people who "served." Why did they show up bright and early on a Saturday morning to bring cake or cookies to a church bake sale that was raising money for some charity? It looked like drudgery, unnecessary obligation and a complete waste of a beautiful morning.

My dislike of service developed into an attitude of cynicism and snobbery. In my mind, the idea of service translated, at best, into doing some kind of volunteer work and, at worst, to a kind of servitude—an impoverished state of mind shared among do-gooders hoping to claim a place in heaven. I felt disdain for "those people," believing they were just trying to look better than the rest of us.

That was the perspective I brought to the service path!

It's taken me years to really understand what service is and what it's not. When I first started coaching with Steve I was like an immigrant in a foreign country. Not only was I unable to speak the language of service, I also didn't relate to, connect with or understand it. And I certainly couldn't do it or be it.

Every time the word "service" was used in our coaching sessions, I tried to ignore or somehow skirt around it. In part I was frustrated because I wasn't actually sure what I was supposed to do. And Steve's attempts to get me to understand service still weren't working because I had so much resistance to it. But he kept at it, offering a simple prompt (again and again) to wear me down and wake me up:

"Ask yourself," Steve would say, "'How can I help someone?' That's service."

*

At the time I often wondered what the hell I'd gotten myself into. Hiring a coach who believed that service was the way to prosperity? But the more I got to know Steve over the years, I realized he wasn't just serving in his professional life. He was modeling living service in his personal life as well.

His *whole life* was built on service.

Today when I work with coaches who are new to this approach, I encourage them to be patient. I tell them about my own initial resistance and confusion. The concept of "service" gets thrown around like everyone knows what it means, but most of us don't—including many coaches. I only began making progress along this path once I slowed down and got clarity by consciously testing out my own understanding of service.

When I thought I was "serving" someone, I asked myself:

- Am I attached to the idea of getting this person as a client?
- Am I "serving" but (wink-wink) really *selling*?

- Is this actually all about me rather than the other person?

Eventually I was able to see how serving worked (and when it didn't). How I felt about an interaction served as a gut check as to whether or not I had a hidden agenda. When I felt I was being disingenuous—not just with someone else, but also with *myself*—I tweaked and re-adjusted the way I served, and I got real-time feedback from my prospects, clients and coach. This was an ongoing process.

I was also inspired by other coaches who served to create clients. I talked to them about their experiences and immediately put what they were doing to the test. Over time, I was delighted to see my understanding deepen as I practiced helping others and gaining insights into what service truly means.

The process continues to this day!

By staying open to what's going on both inside and outside of yourself, your intellectual understanding will begin to integrate with your practice, and service will feel more and more natural.

6

My Sneaky Social Self

One of the most enlightening and useful distinctions I learned along the service path to coaching success was the difference between my social self and my professional self. Clients and prospective clients want a coach to be a true, strong, compassionate professional. And coaches themselves feel better about their work when it takes place in a professional context. Even though these ideas made perfect sense to me, I wasn't aware of how deep my social conditioning was.

I mean, my social self was sneaky as shit.

She would come out of nowhere, contorting me into a rabid people-pleaser, pretending to be interested in other people but with really only one thing in mind: getting clients.

Maybe you have your own version of this social self?

My social self attended choice networking events trying to look professional in dress-for-success outfits, tastefully accessorized from hoop to heel in hopes of attracting my ideal client. She pasted on a toothy grin and impersonated a bobble-head, nodding in vigorous agreement with whomever she was speaking to, hoping to gain their interest and trust just long enough to pitch her AH-MAZING business!

My social self would sidle up to a friend or acquaintance and offer a coaching session not to truly serve and help that person, but to have them see how incredible I was so they would know that they *had* to work with me. When my social self wasn't sure what to charge a prospective client, she'd say things like, "What fee sounds reasonable to you? What's your budget? Let's make this work for both of us!"

Or when she finally met a prospective client for an hour-long coaching conversation, she would spend the first twenty minutes socializing and the next twenty minutes trying to manipulate the conversation back into a professional coaching session. The final twenty minutes? Well, she never confirmed that the person had set aside a full hour. So, at around forty minutes into the hour, she'd be surprised when the prospect would say,

"Oh, my God! I have to leave early to pick up my kids from soccer! I so appreciate your time! Thank you! You're amazing!"

The problem is that my social self (and yours too) is

self-serving, only interested in appearances. How do others see me? Are they impressed? Do I look intelligent? Experienced and highly competent? My social self was impersonating a professional type that I imagined people would want to hire.

It turns out that people don't hire an image. In fact, they intuitively know not to *trust* an image.

To put it simply: I was playing a role that no one was buying.

7

From Fake Pro to Legit

Before I understood the distinction between my social and professional selves, I had never thought of my professional self as the *real* version of me—something my coach had suggested I do. In fact, I thought the exact opposite: my so-called professional self was really just a fake. It was me way back in the 80s, fresh out of law school, newly sworn in as a member of the Bar. Anxious to be taken seriously by experienced lawyers and prospective clients, I did my best to emulate my male mentors and the lawyers I observed in the courtroom.

I still have a picture of me standing outside the Daley Center, the circuit court in downtown Chicago, proudly dressed for professional success in a polyester bow tie blouse with shoulder pads, a shiny suit jacket with shoulder pads, and a vinyl raincoat—also with shoulder pads (the 80s were the worst fashion decade of the twentieth century). I sported a Farrah Fawcett shag haircut and carried a legal briefcase stuffed with professional accessories: legal pads, black pens and business cards.

I was "suited up"—more prepared to play nose guard for the Chicago Bears than to appear for a simple, uncontested motion in court.

That was my idea of "professional."

Flash forward twenty-plus years. I was still carrying around colossal confusion about what it meant to be a professional, mixing odd social behaviors with attempts to be the expert.

My coach could see that, and thank god *he* could, because I was blind to it.

He came up with an ingenious way of *showing* me my social self in action.

Steve asked me to forward him my email exchanges. He knew how insidious that social self could be, and he wanted to help me ferret it out so it didn't get the better of me.

At first I thought this review was overkill. I was a mature woman who at least knew how to *sound* professional (even if my past fashion style was admissible evidence that I couldn't *dress* professionally). But I took his recommendation and sent him my emails for his review.

Immediately, they came pouring back with bold, red

comments everywhere, pointing out where I had fallen into my social self. I felt like I'd regressed back to those school days when I was sure I'd aced the writing assignment but then gotten my paper back corrected within an inch of its life.

Steve would highlight a sentence or phrase and write things like, "Can you see how you're being pleasing and overly friendly here?" or, "Can you be clearer, less vague, and more direct with your offer?"

Some more specific examples:

- I'd offer a coaching session to someone and then act like I had lots of time open so I could accommodate their schedule. "I'm available most days this week! Just let me know what works best for you!" In other words, I was over-accommodating and vague all at once. Far better to define some parameters and keep it simple and direct: "I have Friday at 3 p.m. or next Wednesday at 9 a.m. Which time would you like? Please plan on sixty minutes and we'll have a great conversation."
- My message was overly solicitous (which I confused with serving). "I'd love to get together and hear how I can help you! [emoji heart] Working with parents and their

concerns about their kids is my specialty!! [emoji thumbs up] I've walked my own path with that worry and struggle so I totally understand how you feel!!! [emoji kissing smiling face]" I learned to drop the fawning and pretense along with the exclamation points and emojis and asked myself, what is my real intention when I connect with someone? Is it about them liking me? Or me helping them? So instead I'd go with something like, "Let's talk further about your worry over your son. We'll slow down the conversation and start getting you some clarity and peace of mind. Let me know if you'd like to do that."

I took another stab at it, as if that same teacher from school had given me the chance to improve my grade. I revised my messages, sending them back to Steve for a second, then a third time, and for each he'd work with me to whittle away at the social self's influence. Gradually it became clear to me: my social self's voice was scattered throughout my communications, signaling loud and clear that I was trying to win someone over rather than serve them. I was engaging in a "role reversal" in which *I* was the one needing something from my prospect rather than showing them that I could be of service and help *them.*

When I finally cut through all the layers of fake, I started to see that my true professional self—the authentic version of me minus all the posing and effort—was perfectly designed for service. This is when I began to experience a true sense of power, an innate feeling of ease and competency, the kind that comes when you put on your real clothes, literally and metaphorically, and stop worrying about how others perceive you. When this happens, a natural energy bubbles up, giving you access to your wisdom, humor, caring—and to no BS responses, which means you don't censor yourself. You're not afraid of being direct and saying what needs to be said but in a way your client can hear. For example, if a client is cancelling her coaching calls because she's so busy, I might point out that the very thing we'd work on, her over scheduled life, would be the very thing that would keep her from coming to our calls. What date/time will she prioritize so she can count on herself to follow through? You leave your ego and imaginary needs out of the mix. At this level there's no pretense, just a direct and powerful connection.

This is the real professional self who shows up to serve.

8

Another Piece of the Professional Puzzle: No Downside

Once I discovered the stealth of my social self, I worked hard to keep her at bay. I turned into a social self cop, relentlessly self-monitoring for any signs of that pushy, needy, it's-all-about-me behavior. I held steadily to that line between professional and social, afraid that if I weren't vigilant, I'd find myself tricked once again by my crafty social self. This led to me being on constant alert, which was draining, but I had yet to find a better way.

Until one day, Haley, a client and coach who was growing her business, didn't renew with me. She had made great strides and was ready to go it on her own. She promised that if she needed help, she'd return.

For my own part, I knew she could get stronger in her enrollment and coaching. That is, there was still more we could do together, but for now she felt complete, and

I respected that. We parted ways.

The problem I had was that we were both planning on attending an upcoming event, and my mind kept churning with thoughts about how I should interact with her at it.

I'm not her coach anymore, nor am I her friend. Should I be friendly? Social? Should we go to dinner together? If I'm chummy with her, will that mean I've crossed the line into social land? And if I do that, maybe she'll conclude that I can't really help her anymore!

The event was an entire month away, so I eventually pushed my fearful thoughts aside, sure that something would come to mind before then.

On the opening morning of the conference, the first person I saw in the room was Haley. She was bubbly and smiling and wanted to talk with me. I stayed guarded, trying to look comfortable, but my thoughts were racing: *Cross the line? Don't cross the line? Social? Professional?*

I could barely focus. The social self cop was back!

During the morning break, I took a walk outside, trying to get a grip. There was no way in hell I was going to spend the next three days feeling mentally and emotionally paralyzed. I gave myself a good talking to:

Why can't you just be genuinely friendly toward her?
I can't! If I'm super friendly it might ruin my

professional relationship with her.

What's with the guard you have up? Stop it!

But she'll think we're buddies and realize I'm not the person to help her!

And so on and so on. Back and forth I argued with myself until I realized it was time to go inside and I still hadn't discovered the best course of action. I only knew one thing for certain: I wasn't willing to continue this inner conflict. If being friendly and kind toward Haley would deny me the opportunity to coach her at some future point—so be it.

Living Service ❤ 33

For the remainder of the conference, I was relaxed, laughing with her and getting to know the other participants. I spent time listening to a challenge Haley was experiencing—not as a coach but as a caring person. It was such a relief to just be real! A few weeks after the conference, I received a text from her, asking if we could work together again.

I relayed this story to my coach, describing the time-wasting, energy-draining, crazy-making angst I had put myself through. Had he ever experienced confusion on how to interact with a past client?

He had, and he assured me that any time he became overly focused on how he was coming off to others he created problems that didn't even exist.

Then he said the most obvious, sweetest thing, a simple observation that helped me find the middle ground, the overlap between my social and professional selves, and it changed the way I show up as a professional coach.

"Melissa," he said, "I have found over time that there is no downside to friendliness."

Hearing those sublime words, I wanted to weep.

No downside—only an upside—to friendliness.

No need for ongoing vigilance.

In my effort to stay in my professional lane, I had squeezed all the friendliness out, fearing there'd be a disadvantage or pitfall, as if expressing warmth and kindness would open the proverbial floodgates for my social self to sabotage me. It didn't. It opened the door for real, human connection.

Infusing friendliness back into my coaching relationships melted away my tension and erased the cool distance that being "all business" created. This friendliness was a warm, caring feeling between two humans with no ulterior motive—unlike the pleasing done by my social self, which came from a place of neediness and attachment to getting a client. Friendliness signified that *the door was always open*, and if and when Haley (or any other prospect or past client for that matter) was ready to return, she would know she was welcome.

What's fundamental to a successful coaching relationship?

The relationship.

A professional one filled with warmth, kindness and connection.

9

The Year I Set My Hair on Fire

My sales system—a.k.a., me blindly thrashing around with a vague understanding of service, which *still* didn't resonate with me—wasn't working. After two-and-a-half years of clumsily serving others by giving and giving and hoping prospects would work with me, I wanted a clear-cut approach to sales.

So I changed directions. I intentionally stepped off the service path and set out in search of what I hoped would be the path to prosperity. I hired a new coach, one who combined a pragmatic sales approach with a brilliant ability to diagnose his prospect's problems and create high-paying clients.

I later dubbed this experience "The Year I Set My Hair On Fire and Jumped Off a Cliff."

Here I was, still playing pee-wee football, and what do I do? I hire an NFL coach. I wasn't just outside of my comfort zone—I was way out of my league!

This was my year of small wins and epic failures. I grew (and aged) exponentially, believing that I'd create dazzling breakthroughs if I ran hard enough at my obstacles.

A local therapist referred one of his family members to me for coaching. During the enrollment video call, I pulled out all of my tools: my powerful discovery questions, my well-rehearsed coaching proposal and my high-fee, badass coach persona—that is, my Midwest version of motivational coach Mel Robbins with a dash of Oprah and a pinch of Brené!

But when the conversation ended, I had fallen flat. My prospective client wasn't feeling it. Instead he looked resistant and shut down. I hadn't answered any of his concerns, nor did he know how to help himself, other than to get as far away from me as possible. My badassery had backfired and my ego-sideshow had taken the main stage, ensuring that this prospect (and the referring therapist) would never again respond to my emails.

Sure, I had spoken all the "right" words, but behind those words my intention was loud and clear. It was all about me, my fancy script and impressing people. I knew it and my prospective client felt it.

By the end of the year-long experiment my conversations still felt forced and mechanical, and I knew I wasn't ready for the coaching NFL, that upper echelon of highly paid coaches who make a big impact. But having worked consistently on my personal development for over twenty years, I couldn't understand *why*. Why wasn't I already in this league? I'd witnessed coaches with less experience than me having far greater success! What more did I need?

In my efforts to answer this question, I headed off in yet another direction. I signed up for a program on how to sell my coaching from the stage.

10

The Heart of the Matter

Looking back, I see it was a detour that had to be taken. I was convinced that there was an enrollment system that guaranteed easy clients and money—the "1-2-3 System" for client creation. Social media is littered with advertisements for seven-figure coaching businesses, replete with testimonials from happy, relaxed coaches enjoying their streams of income while sunbathing on soft, white beaches and sipping high-octane cocktails. Why would I continue to flounder trying to serve prospects when there were systems that *delivered*?

I attended a week-long training with approximately a hundred other entrepreneurs learning how to structure our pitches so that people would want to buy our products and services. Towards the end of that week, each participant had a laser feedback session with the mastermind behind the program, ensuring we'd be set up for success!

The sell-from-the-stage guru wasn't dazzled by my pitch.

"You need to organize your presentation in a certain sequence to play on the listeners' emotions," he said, "triggering them to buy in order to release that emotional buildup."

It was the first time I'd heard the rationale behind the sequencing. I'd thought it had to do with the pitch sounding better, flowing better, somehow becoming more alluring so that the client would be enticed to buy. I was told instead that it served people to heighten their emotions—and then release them so they would buy.

The content of what I was saying was important, but even more important was my timing and the emotional . . . well, *manipulative power* of my pitch.

So I'd found the thing I was looking for: a formula that needed to be strictly adhered to in order to deliver results. It had nothing to do with connecting with someone or me helping them first; it had to do with a sales technique. I had swung the pendulum from an internal stance of *giving* to an external system of *getting*—through manipulation. A prospect's decision to work with me had nothing to do with them experiencing my coaching and *knowing* I could help them. It had to do with how well I played them.

Right then, I *knew*.

I knew I didn't want to work a system to get clients. I didn't want to bombard them with clever questions that backed them into a corner. I didn't want to find just the right sequence of phrases that would trigger their "buy" response. And I didn't want to convince anyone they couldn't handle their life without me.

I realized I'd been so busy trying to find the thing outside of me that would generate money that I'd become blinded to the dynamics that create prosperity. I wanted a profitable coaching practice that was based on honesty and trust from the beginning. One based on great coaching that changed lives. And one based on love, caring and human connection—the core of service and the heart of prosperity.

PART II: LEARNING SERVICE

The only person who is educated is the one who has learned how to learn and change.

~ Carl Rogers

11

Learning to Learn

At first, I blamed my struggles to become a successful coach on my lack of a business background. I had stepped away from a full-time career more than twenty years ago, choosing instead to raise my children and make sure the day-to-day responsibilities of our family life were being cared for.

In other words, I'd been out of the game for too long and was missing certain essential business skills. Clearly, I reasoned, this was the cause of my setbacks.

I shared this discovery with one of my colleagues. He scoffed at the idea.

"What do you mean you have no business experience? You practiced law for a number of years. You helped your husband with his business. And you ran a household, which is all about business: budgeting, purchasing, accounts payable, general operations... Not to mention parenting, which is all about leadership.

Stop selling yourself short!"

I took his remarks to heart. This guy was a straight shooter, and I knew he'd be the first one to tell me if I was lacking the necessary business acumen.

Maybe it was my lack of a professional persona? *This* made sense. I'd worked on differentiating between my social and professional selves, but at this time I was still sorting out how to present myself to the world. Having missed out on all those years inside the business world, I was lacking crucial foundational experiences to draw upon to create a "professional" me.

On the other hand, my coach, Steve, said I could develop that part of myself as I progressed. I could decide who I wanted to be as I created my professional self.

"Everyone has to do it at some point," he said.

To that end I studied other coaches I admired, carefully assessing what it was about them that inspired me. I noticed the honesty, kindness, confidence and humor they each embodied. I had those qualities, too, but that still didn't answer my question of *how* to be a professional coach. I needed some idea of how a professional servant acted, because what I was doing clearly wasn't working at deeply serving and creating clients.

My coach offered the metaphor of a doctor.

"Think and act like a doctor," he would tell me.

"How do they act? Are they hoping to be liked or seen as smart? Are they marketing and branding themselves? Trying to sell something or convince you to be their patient? No! They're focused on helping. They listen, and then they tell you what they recommend. You can be that way, too."

So I worked on pretending to think like a doctor—the ones I knew of whom I liked.

For example, insecure thoughts often popped into my head during initial conversations with prospects. Thoughts like:

Do they like me?

Do I sound like I know what I'm talking about?
Will they hire me?

When this happened I'd immediately go into "doctor mode," which meant disengaging from my internal monologue and getting *present* to the person I was trying to help.

Notice. Redirect. Notice. Redirect.

That is, notice the insecure thought, then redirect my attention away from it and towards the person in front of me.

It became a simple game I played. And it was so much better than believing my thoughts were true just because they flew into my head, not to mention trying to *stop* the panic-inducing ones that struck in the middle of an enrollment call.

Over and over, I practiced bringing myself back to a professional self who was completely focused on the person in front of me. And gradually my self-monitoring faded into the background. I began to feel that whatever ideas a person might be having about me didn't really matter. It didn't matter if they thought I was brilliant or average, relevant or old-school or the most amazing coach on the planet! Besides, I had no idea what they were thinking about me anyway. And, I also started to see that I was probably the only one having negative thoughts about an interaction.

As both service and client creation began to feel more natural, I expected I would finally start feeling relaxed and confident about my work. Instead, as I reached more nuanced levels of professional and personal development, my discomfort *increased*. The striving and effort continued.

Around this time I read a book entitled *Mastery: The Keys to Success and Long-Term Fulfillment* by George Leonard. One line in particular caught my eye:

"Bear in mind that on the path of mastery learning never ends."

WTF?

There was no final destination? No place to get to where I'd find myself wrapped in ease and comfort? My worst fears were confirmed. There was no end to all this, and in order to up my game and develop myself into a real businesswoman and master coach, I would have to keep on learning new things.

Ah! I thought. I've found what's holding me back. Not a lack of business skills, or a professional persona, or service or client enrollment. It was really my dislike of failing—which is to say, my fear of learning and what I thought it meant about me . . .

12

Learning Aversion

I remember the first time I heard the phrase "grow or die."

It bothered me. Only two choices? Why couldn't there be a third choice: "status quo"?

I viewed having to learn as a deficiency, evidence that I wasn't capable. Not knowing something was a bad thing, and failing was even worse. So I tried to hide my ignorance and attempted to quickly learn whatever I felt I needed to know in private and then acting in public as if I had it all together. I felt like a fraud.

At the time, this line of thinking felt reasonable and rational. And at least I could console myself that I was admitting the hard truth about myself.

In her book, *Mindset*, author Carol Dweck talks about the difference between a fixed mindset and a growth mindset. For a person with a fixed mindset, the idea that one needs to learn something implies

imperfection and limited potential. So the *act* of learning brings one face to face with this sense of inadequacy in oneself and creates a vicious cycle of bad feelings and negative self-regard. The telltale sign of a fixed mindset? Trying to prove your abilities and intelligence instead of developing them.

In contrast, people with a growth mindset are open-minded, curious and light-hearted; they're insatiable learners. They may struggle, but despite their ups and downs they continue to prioritize learning. They're willing to stay with it, discomfort and all, because they know the challenges involved in learning something new are temporary, and realizing this allows them to progress more quickly.

Look at small children who delight in playing, laughing and trying anything out. Not getting what they want doesn't mean failure to them. They don't doubt their abilities or work on building their confidence before they start learning. They simply learn all day long! This is important to recognize, because we're all born with this growth mindset but some of us, as our personalities

and egos develop, get stuck in our defended, fixed perspectives and struggle. We end up feeling that needing to learn something implies failure and weakness.

That way of thinking about learning sucks the joy and life out of what we are naturally born to do throughout our lives: LEARN!

And this was the classic fixed mindset I'd brought with me onto the service path.

When I started down that path, I never intended to become a better learner. I had no idea about fixed mindsets or growth mindsets or how my approach to learning was holding me back. And when I read Dweck's book, I didn't suddenly think, "Wow, I have this all wrong! I'm going to live life with a growth mindset!" My shift from a fixed to a growth mindset didn't happen overnight, nor did it come about by me flipping a switch in my mind.

It happened when I let go.

When I let go of having to get it right, be right, or look like I had it all together. When I loosened my grip on self-judgment and set aside my ego instead of defending it. When I started receiving feedback and not taking it personally. When I became more comfortable in the creative space of *not knowing*. The greatest obstacle blocking the path between me and what I wanted to create had been my resistance to learning.

I needed to become *coachable*!

There is a direct relationship between my willingness to learn, the impact I make helping my clients and the income I generate. And being a strong learner (a lifelong learner) is the foundation for building and sustaining a prosperous business, because *every time you transform and grow, your business does, too*. When I truly saw that, being a conscious learner became my priority.

I'd ask myself questions:

- Where am I not being totally honest with myself or my coach?
- Am I making up excuses because I'm afraid?
- Where else can I grow?
- What would be fun?
- What area would I prefer not to venture into because I feel uncomfortable? Let's go there!

My coach told me that if I loved serving, I could create a prosperous coaching business. Otherwise client enrollment would be the hard part of coaching, the very thing I would always avoid. I realized that if I cleared the mental junk around learning I would eliminate my struggle so that *learning to serve* would open up and become more enjoyable.

But who could teach me the basics of learning?

13

H.O.W.

A few years ago, following an intervention, a friend of mine agreed to go to rehab for alcohol addiction. On the way to the airport with his family and the interventionist (the person who would accompany him on the flight and then drive him to the treatment facility) he asked, "How do I do this? I've never done this before. How do I recover and stay sober?"

The unknown. A terrifying image of a future without the safety of an addiction.

His whole life was organized around his addiction; in fact, it had merged into the addiction, leaving no trace of him behind. Now, having said yes to receiving help, life was cracking open—which is scary as hell when your lifeline has been alcohol, a substance your body craves, even demands, a substance you believe will ensure your survival.

But the survivor—the addict—was his fake self, a

fabricated persona he kept on life-support through alcohol. His true self was locked away in solitary confinement.

Now he was cruising down the highway to the airport with his family in tow, supporting him, loving him, cheering on his real self.

That real self was the one who showed up during the intervention, the one who listened to his family's request that he accept the help, the one who connected to those words and whose real wisdom came through, out of nowhere, right on time, in the form of a brave decision:

"I'm going! Yes! Let's do this."

And now he was asking, "How do I do this?"

His question hung in the air for a moment before the interventionist spoke. He knew the answer because he had walked his own path of sobriety.

"All you have to remember is the acronym H.O.W. It stands for 'honest, open and willing.' That's all you have to do. That's how you achieve sobriety."

I first heard this story after my friend was safely on the plane. Those of us who had participated in the intervention had gathered together afterwards to decompress. We had been on a wild ride. The odds had been stacked against us and we'd moved forward with a plan that would only work if everything went perfectly.

Thankfully, it did.

It had been a long day and the emotional triumph of the intervention was waning, leaving an aftermath of exhaustion from jangled nerves. My friend's question—"How do I do this?"—reverberated inside me. It humbled and awed me, touching something deep down because it was so human and real and raw. And at the same time, the simplicity and profundity of the interventionist's answer seeped into my being. Truth always does. It finds its way right to the very core, where it heals and catalyzes your soul. Yet for some reason I could not quite find the words to say why the exchange had impacted me so deeply. I could only feel the staggering implications of what had been said. Words would have to come later.

And then life went on. My friend went to rehab, and I got back to my life and work. But the story kept revisiting me, sending me on an inner search-and-rescue mission. There was meaning in it for me, but I couldn't yet see it.

14

Got Courage?

And then I saw it.

It takes courage to raise your hand and say, "I want help! I want out! How do I set myself free?"

Where in my life had I failed to raise my hand? Where had I kept my real self under lock and key? Seemingly safe? Projecting some false persona and keeping the real ME behind bars?

Too many places to count. I'd missed opportunities, sold myself short, made excuses, attacked and defended, held back and waited. It was a case of arrested development caused by fear of making mistakes and failing—or even of succeeding.

I needed a new way; the old one wasn't working.

If my friend could step into the unknown to learn to create sobriety using H.O.W. as his guide, I could certainly do the same with my "unknowns."

For years I had been asking, "How do I grow my

coaching business? How do I get clients?"

In my personal life the questions had been, "How do I have a better relationship with myself? My husband? Family and friends?"

I made some half-hearted attempts on both fronts, a few moves that weren't too scary, but never did I *go for it!* I wanted a clear path, a step-by-step process of the right way to do things before I fully engaged. I was looking for something "out there" so I could stay safe "in here." I had wanted to learn in a way that didn't require my active participation or my own transformation. I wanted learning to be easy.

My friend showed me a different way when he started on his path to sobriety. For life to be different, I had to *learn* differently, and to do that my real self had to show up. I had to be:

Honest.
Open.
Willing.

Ironically, this new way of learning—this new growth mindset—felt, at times, like dying. *I* wasn't dying, but my ego was. At least, it was softening, bit by bit, as the stories that kept it alive began to fade. For instance, if a client was struggling during a coaching session and it appeared he wasn't making any progress, I'd work even harder at trying to find the perfect

HONEST. OPEN. WILLING.

questions to ask or suggestions to make to solve his problem. I'm all for hanging in there with my clients, but my ego was in the mix. I didn't want to look like I didn't have the answer because wouldn't that mean I wasn't a very skillful coach? What if he didn't think I was worth it or believed he had made a grave error in hiring me? With a growth mindset, I realized that, if I was lucky, every client interaction would provide a new learning for me! If my questions weren't useful, what did the client see? What might help them? I could ask. And I did. Often, the client knew exactly what he needed to bring more clarity. And then the conversation would continue because their own wisdom had come through. I learned that I didn't have to have all the answers. I was serving not saving someone!

Or I would go back and listen to my own recorded coaching conversations with my coach. One particular session, I noticed that I kept trying to interrupt him. He wasn't having any of that. He kept talking and I kept trying to get a word in edgewise. I stopped the recording. What was going on? I realized that during the session, I was thinking: "I know this." "I've heard him tell me this a million times!" "I've got this!" I started laughing because I heard—loud and clear—that I wasn't being coachable. At our next session, I told him about my discovery, and that moving forward I would stay open to what he was saying and listen to it like it was the first time I had heard it. More learning! More ability to grow!

I was leaving behind the fixed mindset that told me learning was uncomfortable and challenging. How did I do this? I prioritized learning and actively looked for things I didn't understand. And then I'd engage with them. For instance, I'd bring an enrollment call that I wasn't sure how to handle into a session with my coach and we'd talk it through. My learning deepened and the rationale behind why I was doing what I was doing began to make sense. In the past, I would have never told my coach about the call, concerned he would wonder why, at this stage of my development, I was still working on the basics. And in my personal life, I made a commitment that whenever I was in a conversation with my husband and I started to argue a point about why I was right, I'd stop. And then I'd listen to him and say, "You could be right." Why? Because *he could be right!* And what if I could learn something from him? Consistently, I did. He knew more about business than I had ever given him credit for. Now I had two coaches!

I began to feel lighter and freer, and to see new opportunities for expansion.

At the same time, I had to be careful not to turn H.O.W. into a technique or a thing to tick off, like a pilot's "before-take-off" checklist.

Honest? Check. Open? Check. Willing? Check.

No.

I had to BE IT. NOT do it.

Which took time and focus and practice.

15

Where Had I Not Been HONEST?

My dishonesty occurred at both the conscious and unconscious levels. It was conscious when I pretended to be more accomplished than I was (because I felt threatened by other coaches and secretly jealous of their successes). Dishonesty also had me glossing over problems when talking with my coach, fearing he would judge me for needing coaching yet again on the same old tired issue which I had yet to figure out.

My dishonesty on the unconscious level was sneakier, at times masking itself as insecurity, which showed up in the form of anxiousness, irritation or self-doubt, tugging at my skirt hem like a small child trying to get my attention. Behind those feelings were lies about myself that held me back. Beliefs about being incapable of succeeding, about not being "good enough," about just being a certain way and unable to change.

When I finally dared to look—when I was finally

honest with myself—I uncovered truths that lightened that illusory load.

I realized that because I am inherently an honest person, dishonesty was dragging me down. Dishonesty came in the form of my ego, which I was constantly trying to shore up. I was tired of trying to put on a front, looking like I had it together when talking with colleagues and friends. Or there was also the habitual thought that felt real—even though I repeatedly disproved its truth—that maybe I just couldn't get this business to succeed. This was a constant lie I leveled at myself and then desperately struggled not to believe. It was an internal wrestling match—me against me—insuring I'd be the loser if I didn't pull myself out of the ring.

Understanding who I really am turned out to be a good thing because it finally drove me to ask for help and *take it*, just as my friend had done during the intervention. Staying honest with myself and with my coach increased the speed of my learning, and I felt so much better! When I saw the power of honesty, like the old adage, *honesty is the best policy,* I decided I'd be real instead of hiding behind my ego. It was a decision, an internal commitment to show up differently. For instance, I decided that in conversations with my coach I'd share exactly how I felt rather than try to look good.

I brought old fears to our calls to question them, and I saw recurring thought patterns that no longer served me. I opened up to learning from other coaches and to attending their programs, too, which my coach encouraged. I hung in there with myself, taking a kinder, more self-loving stance rather than trying to edit out my humanness and be perfect (not only stressful but impossible). And I realized that my state of mind needed to be cared for just like my physical body. I started my day reading inspiring books or listening to uplifting audios combined with movement, whether it was stretching or taking a walk outside. Staying honest with myself and with my coach increased the speed of my learning. My old, fixed mindset was gradually superseded by a new self that looked forward to tackling new challenges and learning new things.

I could still slip. Once I confided to my coach that I was making "poor progress." He rebutted with, "You've got that wrong! It's time to catch up to your current self-concept!"

And I realized he was right. I *had* changed. I'd been operating from a whole new level of growth. Honesty cracked my ego's protective, prideful shell. One side effect of this was that it opened me up to conversations with other coaches who were also afraid of failing.

Pride was the poison, honesty the cure.

And honesty flowed into my coaching, making it possible for me to share my own setbacks and mishaps with clients when it seemed like it would serve them to do so. This allowed them to relax, to see that nothing was wrong with them or their progress. They were right on target!

And—I was slowly starting to see—so was I.

16

How to Be OPEN

I'd closed the door on being open long ago.

Why would I need to be open when I was "right"? The way I'd operated most of my life was to quickly assume that others were wrong or misinformed when their opinions didn't match up with mine. The pivotal moment, the moment when I fell in love with being open, came when my coach challenged me to an experiment:

Listen to a loved one's criticisms without defending yourself.

Now this was a tall order. Usually when I was criticized, I would jab back, making a comment here or a put-down there. But Steve's directions were clear: "Just listen. Say nothing. If you feel a zing or a sting, there's probably some truth there. *Do not say anything.* Let the other person speak, and when they're done, say, 'I can be like that.'"

"Really?" I asked, adding with more-than-slight

sarcasm. "That sounds like fun! Anything else?"

"Yes. *Thank* them."

Oh my God! I couldn't think of anything I'd rather NOT do. But since I was having such an intense, internal reaction, I knew to agree. That reaction was telling me this was an area of resistance that could use some attention.

A few weeks later, the opportunity presented itself. Now this wasn't a major argument; it was what I call a "jab fest," the kind of thing most of us get into with loved ones now and again because we can so easily push each other's buttons. On this particular night my husband came home around eight. We'd both had long days and in fact I was finishing up an email when he came in the backdoor.

"Hi!" I said, without looking up from my laptop. He soon went into the other room and started flipping through tv channels. And as it often goes with these sorts of things, I don't even recall exactly what he or I said that started it up! All I can recall is that familiar feeling of irritation and defensiveness rising up in me as he said one thing or another that I took to be attacks.

But this time, when those all-too-familiar criticisms were leveled at me . . . *I listened*.

Fully.

Because my coach's directions were to shut up, I

wasn't busy thinking of my next response to whatever volley was being lobbed at me. My mind was quiet.

It was a strange, almost out-of-body feeling, by which I mean that I heard what he was saying, but I didn't take it personally. Instead I just watched as irritation, upset and exhaustion played across his face. Even stranger, even though it was all directed at me, I felt for the guy. I remember thinking that I had never kept my mouth shut in these situations, and neither had I listened. I was always too busy thinking of my next response, my comeback comment, my jab.

In silence, I could feel my ego rise up and then die down. I felt compassion for both of us. I could see he was wrapped up in his own thinking—but only because I normally was too.

Finally, the comments ended and I said softy,

"I can be like that."

He looked at me, incredulous. And then he said, "You know, you don't have to be that hard on yourself."

Huh? I couldn't believe what he just said. In the heat of our past arguments, I had been operating from the belief that he was uncaring and mean-spirited when he was being critical of me. But he wasn't. My hurtful stories and judgments about him had hurt me. He hadn't.

Being closed and defensive (in order to protect myself) was the cause of feeling pained and disconnected. Being open (listening with a quiet mind) allowed access to a wellspring of love and compassion.

He looked at me with a smile on his face and asked, "Are you okay? Do you need a hug?"

WTF??? I had *never* been in a disagreement that ended this way. Usually we kept a chilly distance until we got over it.

I knew what Steve would tell me to do. Take the hug.

I did.

I also took the lesson.

17

Willing to Be WILLING?

I hadn't been willing to get into action because I'd been so busy trying to figure things out conceptually *before* taking action. I was always looking for the answer to "how."

How do I get clients?
How much do I charge for my services?
How do I convince people to work with me?
How do I get the confidence to do any of this?

And I wasn't willing to get into action until I'd figured all this out.

Eventually I saw that my questions were more about fear than curiosity. I wasn't willing to take even small steps forward because I was afraid of being unprepared, of falling on my face, of revealing myself to be a failure. So my "how" questions created a buffer between me and the danger involved in striking out in new directions. If I told myself I couldn't move until I'd answered the "how" questions, then

I had a perfectly good excuse for staying where I was.

Once I saw that the only way forward was to be willing—to be honest, to be open, to get things wrong, to move forward *without* the answers—willingness became the wind in my sails.

Willingness created the breakthroughs!

I emceed a local non-profit's charitable fundraiser of two-hundred-plus attendees, the movers and shakers in my town. Of course the last thing I wanted to do was look foolish in front of "important" people and ruin my reputation, but now I was willing to test my mettle and not run from the opportunity.

I coached someone whom I had classified as a pedestal person, someone I considered to be way out of my league. I realized that in doing so I might find out I wasn't qualified or capable—but I also might discover what my coach had been telling me all along: "People are human! They want help. Go help someone!"

I decided to write this book even though at times I wondered whether a million other people couldn't write it better. And what if it spoke to no one?

Willingness was liberating, proving to my ego that no matter what I did and regardless of the outcome, the real me wasn't going to die.

The real me was learning H.O.W.

18

Three Stages of Mastery

Perhaps we'll never know how far the path can go, how much a human being can truly achieve, until we realize that the ultimate reward is not a gold medal but the path itself.

~ George Leonard

With service more firmly under my belt, Steve encouraged me to join his year-long group for coaches who had reached a higher level in client creation through service and who desired to grow into exceptional coaches. We were a small, intimate group of six who met four times a year throughout the U.S., each time spending two days together holed up in hotel conference rooms with the intention of creating transformation in our personal and professional lives. At this point, I had a full roster of clients, was working full-time and thrilled to be making more money than I'd ever imagined making.

I was beginning to see that the speed of my learning was in my own hands, and that if I dared to lay all my cards on the table, positive growth would occur in all areas of my life.

I was ready.

Steve began our meetings by sharing a thought-provoking idea, which in turn sparked lively, introspective discussions that opened our minds to new ways of seeing life. At one meeting, he introduced us to the "Three Stages of Meditation Mastery" designed by the Tibetan Buddhist Monk, Matthieu Ricard. Steve explained how Ricard's simple stages could be applied

to the mastery of all things—including learning and practicing sales through service.

My ears perked up. There were stages to learning?

This particular meeting took place around the time when my relationship with learning was still shifting. I'd been used to operating under the assumption that you either loved learning or you didn't. If you did, you quickly mastered service, applied it effortlessly and with great success, and were then done learning.

Or, if you were like me, you joined the remedial group where the process of learning service unfolded more like the days did for Bill Murray's character in the movie *Groundhog Day*: he was reliving the same day, day after day after day, with no end in sight.

But now Steve was explaining there was a process involved, that there were different stages involved in learning something new.

Ricard's three stages powered up a giant Klieg light, illuminating the brilliant truth of my journey—not the whopper of a story I had been telling myself about being a slow learner or finding reasons why "getting service" was so hard.

I wasn't in a remedial group. I was simply *learning*.
Nothing more and nothing less.

19

The Stages of Service Mastery

#1: Love Your Process

You think you understand the concept of service, but when you go to test it out, it doesn't work.

Welcome to Stage #1. Now what?

Service is simple, right? Just find where people need help and offer your assistance. They'll naturally gravitate into a working relationship with you and everything will magically fall into place.

So why is it so hard to enroll a client? To have a prospect say yes to that coaching conversation you so generously offered? Yes to the proposal you made?

Instead of: "I'll have to think about it" or "I'll get back to you in a week after I get my bonus" or "Let me talk to my partner/financial/investor/astrologer" or "I don't have the money but let me go create it!"

Living Service ♥ 75

And then they vanish, never to be heard from again.

For some of us the challenge may be, "Who do I even invite into a coaching conversation?" Family and friends feel awkward. Online social media posts yield limited responses—even if people love your inspirational quotes, selfies and that live broadcast you made on Periscope while you were hiking the Himalayas.

You may be doing your best to serve, but service isn't working. You either aren't getting any clients, or it takes a Herculean effort on your part to get a few dribbling in.

Your business and YOU feel chaotic.

This means you are firmly at Stage #1 in mastering service.

Let me tell you something now that I *definitely* didn't know at Stage #1, something that makes all the difference.

Chaos is the seat of creativity. It's where it ALL happens. Author and master coach Michael Neill writes that "creativity starts with nothing and then it begins to take form, turning into something." Back then this struck me as a great concept, but at the time I wasn't happy with the "something" I had created or the chaos I was experiencing. I didn't even see myself as a creative person. Instead, when I was firmly in Stage #1, I felt like a massive ball of confusion and uncertainty; if I was lucky, I felt, maybe I was moving forward. Some coaches handle this uncertainty with lightheartedness and grace. Others (including yours truly) experience struggle and discomfort with the "not knowing" and the lack of stellar results at this point in the journey.

The graceful ones have a secret: they love the process of learning to create clients. Their so-called failures are opportunities to grow, not give up. They trust that at some point the desired result will come—the prospect will become a client—but until then they are engaged in learning. And this isn't just the kind of learning that involves reading a new book or attending a seminar. This kind of active learning means taking action, testing out new ideas, reflecting on what's worked and what hasn't. Learning in this context also means *staying on the path.* Sure, the process might get tiring at times. Even the "graceful" among us coaches might wish they were making greater gains. *But . . .* then we see it's futile, "future" thinking that's bringing us down. We come back to where we're at: the present moment, and we take the next step along the service path. We continue to learn.

More than that, we fall back in love with learning.

The coaches who struggle are the ones focused on producing quick outcomes versus steady progress based on a growth mindset. When these coaches inevitably fall short of their goals, they judge themselves relentlessly. They see their failures as somehow reflecting who they are rather than merely the result of a misguided approach for acquiring clients. Learning is the last thing on their minds.

This was my own experience. I spent so much time looking for the guaranteed, fail-safe, "right" method for serving and acquiring clients that I neglected my own growth along the path. I was continually trying to figure it out, but I was never going to because there is no "it"— no standard, checklist approach to enrolling clients through service. You'll never find an external strategy to service because service isn't an external strategy; it's an internal stance, a way of being which leads to creative, intuitive ways of helping others. It doesn't happen through developing a sales funnel or implementing proven sales tactics guaranteed to increase your conversion rate.

Service is a creative endeavor. Just as coaches and the prospects they work with are myriad and diverse, so too are the different ways of serving. Service requires that you move beyond your analytical, strategic, systems thinking about "getting" clients and learn to create with your entire head and heart. Then, and only then, will your level of service deepen. And *that* results in people wanting to work with you.

Until I heard about Ricard's Three Stages of Mastery, my creativity was inaccessible to me because I experienced learning and self-judgment as inextricably tied together. With the understanding that learning is a process came a great sense of relief. I could let myself off the hook! Now I was left with three simple stages of ongoing practice.

The path was doable.

In Stage #1 you need a strong desire and willingness to stay committed and conscious on the path, because growth often isn't detectable at this point.

Frequently, a coach at this stage will fall for the "What's wrong with me?" story, or wrongly interpret her limited results as a sign that "service doesn't work." Reaching this conclusion, she's likely to head in another direction, unintentionally adding another stage along the way.

Or rather, a detour.

20

The Stages of Service Mastery

The Detour

Detour thinking sounds something like this:

"What do you mean *serve* someone before they pay me!? I don't have all the time in the world to coach people for free!! When does the money start flowing in?"

Or . . .

"I understand service; it's a beautiful thing, and I love helping people. But how do I know when to *stop* serving and have people *pay* me? I hear internet marketing drives results, and I need to make money, so maybe I just need to switch gears and go in that direction for a while . . ."

The plan being that when you bail from the service path, you'll begin "working on your business." Ironically, I have found this to be the very thing that won't create clients. Working on your business typically translates into ramping up your networking by handing out business cards like Halloween candy, asking family and friends for referrals, developing an SEO strategy, learning how to sell from the stage, and building your social media footprint. The goal being "getting yourself out there!"

None of these strategies is wrong, but without the mindset of service as your strong foundation, creating clients will remain a distant dream, because people will feel targeted, manipulated and sold. And that's what happens when most coaches get off the service path. Instead of coming from "Let me help," they move into "I need clients!" Prospects can feel the difference, and they run.

Service has to be solid inside of you. The latest and greatest marketing doesn't replace a sincere desire to help someone. Without service in your heart, it's obvious to everyone what you're up to. The goal of helping people slides into a process of hatching plans.

Sometimes coaches need to leave the path and pursue those "guaranteed" routes to prosperity. There is a plethora of consultants who aim to help you harness the power of LinkedIn, Facebook, YouTube, Instagram, etc., to build brand recognition, grow your following, drive leads and boost your conversion rates. Or "use marketing automation to get more clients easily and achieve the freedom you desire overnight!" as one consultant pitched me. And it's enticing! Why should I work so hard learning service when there are easier ways?

As I shared above, I left the service path in pursuit of these so-called simple and guaranteed strategies, drawn by the allure of creating a successful business "in ninety days." Why wait *years*?

My detour delayed my progress, but I needed to find out for myself that playing off of people's emotions to sell my coaching didn't feel good—or work. There was an emptiness about this frenetic obsession of trying to get ahead. I started to see the importance in slowing down, connecting and caring enough to help. I began to feel the real value, for me and for my clients, in building trusting, solid relationships.

So I returned to the service path—you always can too—which eventually brought me to the next stage of mastery.

21

The Stages of Service Mastery

#2: Own Your Progress

You've arrived! You're killing it! Sharing wild success stories with your friends and family about amazing enrollment conversations where you stayed in the lead, closing a new client at your higher fee! Your optimism is running high! And then—

It's not.

You're not crushing it.

You have a long string of perceived failures—people saying no to your proposals or not responding to your messages or emails.

You're flip-flopping back and forth about the coaching fees you should charge, feeling doubtful and indecisive.

You're sailing the stormy service seas like an

emotional pre-teen, flying high one minute and desperately low the next.

This second stage is a mix of excitement and frustration. It's like the old Jim McKay slogan on ABC's *Wide World of Sports*: "The thrill of victory and the agony of defeat!"

In Stage #2, you still wish mastering service would go faster but you're not going to get off the path. Lesson learned. If you have a coach, she'll keep pointing out that you're doing great—"Hell, you're in Stage #2!"—but you won't necessarily *feel* great. Why? Because you thought that you already "got" service, so what's with all these failed enrollment calls? Or the nagging question you ask yourself: "Who else can I coach?"

But you decide to take your coach's word, and you stay open so you can learn from the problems hindering your progress.

"You don't know what you don't know" sums up Stage #2. There will always be gaps in your knowledge, and Stage #2 requires that you hang in there and find those gaps, those pesky blind spots where service breaks down and you're not even seeing it. A successful coach, someone who powerfully serves to create clients in their own thriving business, can help you see those gaps and fill them—they can help you get out of your own way and strengthen your service.

Stage #2 is still a hot mess of creative chaos, but *you* are different. You're feeling more comfortable with the discomfort of "not knowing." The messiness of creativity doesn't give you pause. Learning isn't so bad after all, because every time another blind spot is revealed, you see the next step to take, and your learning progresses.

For example, you might be having multiple conversations with a prospect and the person still isn't asking to work with you. Some questions to ask would be:

- Has the prospect experienced a shift, a new insight?
- Are you staying in the lead, letting your prospect know how you work and next steps?
- Has your service turned into sales so that you're talking about the value of coaching instead of coaching the prospect so they experience a change in how they see their world?

Maybe you believe it should only take one conversation to create a paying client, so at the end of your first session you make a proposal which gets turned down, or the prospect objects to it for some reason. In such a case you might be rushing to get a client rather than slowing down so that your prospect can experience the impact of your coaching on a personal level rather than a conceptual one. They have to see that their own life's getting better before they hire you.

Stage #2 involves constant redirection, bringing your head and heart back to service while consistently coaching, running game film with your coach (revisiting your every "play" in your approach to coaching) and staying open to more.

Because there's always more to see. More to learn. More to grow.

22

The Stages of Service Mastery

#3: You've Got This!

Finally, you've reached Stage #3. You're taking yourself and the speed of your progress less seriously. Learning is enjoyable, even something you look forward to, and it continues in richer, more nuanced forms.

My coaching practice had reached maximum capacity. I had a packed schedule, working with approximately eighteen clients and conducting ongoing enrollment conversations. I was finally breaking multiple six figures, feeling thrilled about the service I provided and delighting in my clients and our work together. I didn't want to take my foot off the accelerator since it felt so good to experience consistent, strong results from my efforts.

I was loving it all, but the pace was challenging to

sustain. One of my colleagues, master coach Karen Davis, approached her business in a more relaxed, slowed down way, working with fewer clients and generating more income. Karen was matter of fact. *If you create more space in your calendar, you'll serve at a higher level and the clients you create will be your ideal clients.* Less hustle? It seemed so counterintuitive but clearly she knew something I didn't. What would happen if I walked instead of ran?

Was there a deeper level to service that I hadn't seen yet?

I began experimenting, cutting back on client creation, freeing up more time for myself personally. I stopped scheduling client calls back-to-back, allowing for ample time between sessions to clear my mind by taking a walk, reading or just hanging out. My coach had repeatedly advised me to do this, but now I knew why. With less "doing," my mind quieted down and my level of service rose. My actions became more thoughtful because I had more spaciousness in my life. I had more inspired ideas that shifted how I did things.

- Instead of hurried emails or text/messages, I took my time crafting responses that would make a difference.
- Rather than speed-reading emails and texts to

be efficient, I gave them the attention they deserved and thus stopped misinterpreting them.
- Instead of somewhat randomly sending a book to a client (here's your book-of-the-month!) I'd send one more thoughtfully, one I knew might shed light on a concern or area of their life they wanted to enhance.
- I made it a habit to take time before each session to think about my client, connecting with them even before the session began.

"You can always improve," my coach would say. And I did. As I got better at providing a higher level of service, more people referred me, knowing that their friends, family members and colleagues were in good hands.

My coaching shifted from teaching concepts to helping my clients access their own knowing. What new insights could they uncover by connecting with their own learning process and innate wisdom? When I remained fully present to something my client was sharing instead of thinking about how I would respond, a deeper transformation occurred for them.

Preparing for enrollment conversations and knowing what I would offer a prospect who wanted to continue allowed me to stay in the lead when it was time to answer the question, "What does it look like to work with you?" Being clear, direct and keeping it simple, made decision-making easier for a prospect.

At Stage #3 along the service path, service feels natural; it becomes second nature. With all that accumulated practice, service is no longer what you "do" to create clients, it's who you are. It's a way of living. You no longer have to think about "how to serve" because, as my own coach would tell me: "It's in you. And it never goes away."

This is the stage where you hear some coaches talk about being able to create clients at will. They can turn the dial up and add more clients to their practice, or dial it down, enroll fewer clients and (for coaches who want to) create a waiting list.

Stage #3 has a hidden bonus: *your own transformation*. Because service is a place to come from rather than a technique or tool, it requires that you grow internally, transform your insecurities and free yourself up to be more of who you need to be. For instance:

- If your coach persona is the badass boss, you might discover that upgraded service comes from a softening, a more compassionate

approach where you lovingly tell the truth to a client.
- If you're the expert with the wisdom of a sage, a coach with all the "right" answers, directing and advising might take a back seat so you can listen instead from a place of understanding and curiosity and help unearth your client's own authority.
- If you're trying to prove that your coaching "works" in order to convince prospects to hire you, you now see how truly giving without attachment dissolves any subtle resistance from prospects—and more people sign up with you. Of course, in order to do this, you have to be at a stage where you really can give without attachment to the outcome.

The service path will have its way with you, opening your mind and heart to greater clarity and truth, strengthening who you really are, and turning your coaching into an expression of your love.

23

The Service Game

"So how do we play this Service Game?" I asked hesitantly.

"We don't know," laughed Gary. "I was just talking to Dave and we decided to make it up as we go. We wanted to know if you were in."

Dave Schwendiman, Gary Mahler and I met in Steve Chandler's ACS (Advanced Client Systems) school, which teaches coaches how to create a prosperous coaching business through service, not sales. I didn't know them very well, but from the little I did, it seemed like the three of us couldn't be more different. Gary, sporting a cool, surfer image, was a world traveler, loving father and husband. Dave was into CrossFit, his two kids, building businesses and laughing an irresistible, contagious laughter which makes all the sense in the world considering his spirit animal is a unicorn. Both guys were smart, free-spirited, fun-loving and continually finding humor in things I didn't. They reminded me of middle-school boys sharing insider jokes, the kind only they found funny.

I was on the other end of the spectrum. My husband was actively running his own business and my kids were grown adults making their way in the world. I had one focus: proving I could make money as a professional coach. I was serious. Intense. Obsessed. Wishing to be anywhere but here—on my service journey. My progress felt slow and I still wasn't convinced service was all it was hyped up to be.

I was firmly in Stage #2, loving neither learning nor service, but needing to.

I had two reactions upon getting this call from Gary: flattered and confused. Flattered to be invited by two coaches committed to making gains and confused because I didn't know why I was being asked. There were so many other coaches like them: dynamic, extroverted, taking the world by storm. Coaches who were better connected, having started earlier in this profession than I had.

Why me, I wondered?

But I didn't ask, at least not right away, because I didn't want to know if I was the fifth coach on their list of five. I stayed quiet at first. When I finally got up the nerve to ask, Dave replied matter-of-factly that they knew they'd have *fun* at this game but needed someone who was serious about it, someone who would keep them grounded, focused and on track so they wouldn't screw it up.

Well, they had me pegged correctly but for one minor point: I felt an aversion to everything they were proposing.

Games. Service. No rules.

Ugh!

Yet there was something intriguing about the timing of their invitation. I had yet to experience any major breakthroughs generating income through service. I created sporadic clients, but my nagging self-doubts kept both the joy of service and its financial rewards at bay. I was ready for a leap in my progress.

What would it be like to join a small band and learn together? Play a game? Not toil on my own? Learn in a fun-filled, playful and collaborative way along with two guys who didn't take their progress or themselves so seriously? Gary and Dave's whole approach to learning felt foreign to me, but I knew that I needed more of what they had.

24

Playing without Fear

When I accepted their invitation, I felt a fear rise up that I desperately wanted to conceal. I didn't want Gary or Dave to know how anxious I felt about moving coaching conversations to closure, how I had to steel myself each time I stated my fee and waited for a prospect's response.

I needed to get a handle on my fear in order to take full advantage of this opportunity, so I tried reasoning with myself: *What's the worst thing that can happen? I'll be broke for another three months? So what!? I've been broke for years.*

Another fear rippled just beneath the surface, one that had plagued me for a long time, but I did what I had always done in the face of it: I pushed forward.

"Okay. I'm in! But let's figure out what this game is all about, because I can't start playing unless I understand what the hell we're doing." I was slightly irritated and trying to mask my anxiety.

"It's really simple," Gary replied in his upbeat tone. "The basic premise is that we profoundly serve people for the next ninety days. We help them. Become their catalyst for transformation. Listen, ask questions, love them. You name it; whatever we need to do."

"Alright," I said, "but I need something more."

"What is it?"

"I've been doing some version of service for the last few years," I explained. "I've been helping, giving—but it's still not enough. I hold back somehow. I feel it. If I'm really going to serve profoundly, I can't be attached to whatever my fear is. So we have to serve without our fears."

I had hoped that would be the end of the fear discussion, leaving me to sort out my terror in private, but Gary said, "I like it. What's your fear?"

"Uh . . . Well," I quietly confided, trying to sound casual, "I'm afraid if I boldly serve, giving it everything I've got, I'll find out that no one will hire me. No one will want to work with me."

There. It was out. This "I can't make it work" mindset had been eating away at me for years and I had just divulged it to this "happy" guy.

"You're afraid that no one will work with you?"

"Yes, that's it," I replied, defeated before I even started.

"Then it's *ever*!" Gary laughed with enthusiasm.

"What do you mean, '*ever*'?" I responded, feeling touchy and confused by his effervescence. I didn't see what he found so funny in my *very real* fear.

"That's your service game. You will play the game, boldly serving, and you will do it for ninety days, playing full-out, *knowing* that no one will *ever* work with you *ever* again!"

Damn. He was spot on.

But then I wondered: *Could I really play this service game for three months without fear? And if not* now, *then when?*

I knew what it was like trying to serve while holding tightly to my fears. That's how I felt when I first started on the service path. I was extremely uncomfortable, holding back, terrified of making mistakes—and then I beat myself up when I inevitably did. Second-guessing my decisions on what to charge and how to structure engagements added doubt to the toxic mix. The constant stress of trying to control and manage myself and my negative emotions was exhausting.

It had let up a bit over time, but whenever I experienced unwanted results, such as prospects saying "No" or "I'll think about it," I couldn't see what had caused the problem. I couldn't see where my service had weakened. In my doubt-filled moments, I wasn't even sure if service was a real way to grow a business or just another gimmick being sold to coaches.

So my understanding of service needed an upgrade. So did my learning style, and Dave and Gary looked like they were having a hell of a lot more fun on their path. I wanted more of that instead of the dour, resistant approach I'd been taking to learning. I wanted to see whether regaining a bit of humor and having some compassion for myself and others—not to mention being full-on honest with these two guys—would make any difference.

The idea of me starting out the game by letting go of needing anyone to *ever* hire me was brilliant. It immediately took all the pressure off and created a lightness inside of me. I could sense that this game was perfectly set up for me to grow, as long as I played full out.

Now it was Gary's turn. I asked him, "What fear holds you back from powerfully serving?"

Gary admitted to us that, "I need to be liked. Approved of. It stops me every time."

So his service game looked slightly different from mine.

"That's *your* service game!" I gleefully announced. "You will play the game, boldly serving. You will do it for ninety days, and no one will *ever* like you—*ever* again!"

Gary laughed. "I'm in!"

Now it was time to corner Schwendiman.

Dave was ready. He admitted being afraid to strongly call someone on their BS story. This fear stopped Dave dead in his tracks. He held back from being direct and honest in a coaching session because he didn't want to find out that he'd somehow gotten it wrong. His marching orders were to powerfully serve and be willing to get it wrong—*always*.

The game was simple yet challenging. There were no winners or losers. No "me against them." We were there for each other, pooling our mental resources to help each other, giving feedback to one another, testing out new ideas, maintaining a dynamic state of action.

I had never opened up to other coaches in this way before. I'd kept my cards close to my chest, keeping my slip-ups and face plants undercover and learning only from my own coach. Suddenly my playground expanded by two; I was no longer hiding.

We settled on one more rule before starting: each of us had to play the game *without*—not *through*—our fears. Why this rule? Because we intuitively knew that fear was diluting our service.

There's a big difference between playing *through* and playing *without* one's fear.

The former is done by slogging through something while dragging fear-based thinking along like a ball and chain. I'd already been playing that game for a while, and I could attest to the fact that it didn't work. Playing *without* fear meant letting go of it altogether. Leap before you look. In doing so, we hoped, we would unleash service at the profoundest levels.

25

Game On!

And so the game began.

At first I experimented with different ways to be fearless with prospects and my cohort. In many ways, it was simple. When I prioritized 100 percent service as a place to come from, my fear naturally got left behind. There was no room for it. When I felt myself drifting back into being concerned about myself, I'd simply shift my focus back to my prospect.

After all, if they weren't going to hire me (per the rules of the game), then there was no reason for me to pay such close attention to myself and make sure I was getting it "right." Once I got into this mindset, coaching sessions became pure freedom. Whatever I offered to my clients and prospects came from a space of complete service. Saying my fee came easily because I had cultivated the expectation that no one would hire me anyway. And *finally* I could offer it confidently.

Inviting prospects to talk? A no brainer. If they weren't interested, so what? No one would hire me anyway. On to the next!

Doing fearless things around Dave and Gary became a priority for me—things like being honest about how I was feeling or revealing when something went sideways in a coaching session. Or asking for their feedback and being open to hearing it without hurting my feelings. This mindset allowed me to take feedback in rather than dismissing it. I became willing to go try something different and report back to them what had happened.

Whenever I experienced moments of doubt or confusion, or when I just wanted to laugh, Gary and Dave were there.

We had a message thread where we connected multiple times a day. If someone needed a sounding board or coaching, one or all of us would help. We offered words of encouragement, shared triumphs and funny stories of screwups.

Our game had become so much more than serving our prospects and clients. It had morphed into serving each other.

Here's one example of how things played out: I had a few conversations with an entrepreneur who wanted to grow her business, but she was frustrated that it wasn't expanding quickly enough. I could see where she was afraid to move forward and I honestly shared my insight with her. We had a few powerful, slowed-down sessions where I could see the light going on for her. Then she went radio silent when I offered her a final conversation via email. I waited a few days and emailed her again, letting her know that if and when she was ready, I was available to help. I ran game film, reflecting on what had happened, and I couldn't see anything about my actions I would change. I began to second guess myself. Maybe I had come on too strong? So I asked for feedback.

Dave responded:

> I know your service and you'd never come
> on too strong. Direct. Yes. Loving. Yes.
> No need to doubt yourself. Move on.

Gary chimed in. *I agree. Find the next person to help!*

So there it was, once again, my self-doubt clouding my ability to neutrally evaluate but it didn't last for long because I could trust both guys to tell it to me straight. I dropped the doubt and got back into serving, asking the question, *Who's next?* With Dave and Gary on my team, I consistently played at a higher level. My strong commitment to both of them (and to myself) dialed up an unstoppable drive to play full out! Even (and especially) if I fell down, I had to get back up. Prior to joining them, I would muck around feeling uncertain, getting caught in negative stories and believing them to be true, then wasting time when I could have been helping someone else. Our mutual truth-telling helped each one of us get over ourselves and get back into action. Or as Gary would simply put it: "We need to get our heads out of our asses and keep serving!" And we did.

Dave and Gary were my priority and I was committed to their growth and results. As we continued to play, we started referring to each other as our service family. Gary wanted me to review an email to see whether there was any sign of neediness or social self coming through. I did, taking my time to respond thoughtfully and honestly. Dave wanted to discuss a proposal before offering it; Gary and I got on the phone with him. Every time I helped them, I saw something new for myself that grew my effectiveness as a coach who could powerfully serve.

Sometimes our messaging back and forth continued, for me, late into the night because I lived in a time zone two hours ahead of Gary and Dave. There were many nights when I would be in bed and hear my phone vibrate on my nightstand. I'd quietly reach for the phone, hoping not to wake my sleeping husband, so I could respond to a group message. My intense, obsessive serving took our game to another level—which for me made it even more fun and impactful! We were on a mission . . .

The game also shifted my relationship to the idea of learning. Dave and Gary became my role models. They showed me that when levity and love naturally flow, learning and staying in action become easier and more enjoyable the more you practice them. These were things I doubt I would have learned on my own—or at least not nearly as effectively and quickly. Our dynamic had a synergistic effect on our ability to serve that no book or seminar alone could have created.

Even though there was only one rule to our game—

play without fear—I created some additional unwritten rules for myself, things like being light-hearted and laughing when I make a mistake, rather than sliding into seriousness and self-judgment. I consciously relaxed into the space of "not knowing" and saw it for what it really was.

Really, what was going on was that I was actively learning that nothing was wrong with me. Learning infused with fun didn't dilute my lessons or distract me from my goals; in fact, it had the opposite effect. It fueled my desire, my creativity and my productivity.

The best part was listening to Dave and Gary celebrating their victories and envisioning future success. "I just closed a $4K client!" or "I'm a world-class coach!" or "Watch me powerfully serve this prospect and create an apprentice!" Two cool things happened from this. First, I was happy for them. I got excited about their "wins!" And second, they inspired me. If Gary could dream big, I could too. Or if Dave's enthusiasm kept him energized, why couldn't I infuse more of that into my approach? I got caught up in their joy rather than falling into the comparison game. We were all in this together!

Service was no longer a tactical approach to client creation; it was who I was becoming. Playing the game knowing that no one is ever going to hire me allowed me to see service for what it is: genuine love, caring and connection. Putting someone first not because I was supposed to but because I wanted to.

This act of putting someone else's success first not only applied to my prospects and clients but, much to my surprise, to Gary's and Dave's success as well. I started to see the importance of being in a community of like-minded coaches who were dedicated to service, who wanted to help each other and have a good time along the way. Playing this game filled me with hope, strengthened my growth mindset and, for the first time, opened my eyes to the power of service.

Besides it was ridiculous fun!

Then three months passed, and I realized I had broken six figures.

Please note, though: neither this game nor any other guarantees you'll magically break six figures. I'd always get crazy seeing phrases like "Ninety days/Six figures!" being touted on various social media platforms.

No game, no technique and no special script is going to do that for you.

It's your creation. All you.

It wasn't a fluke, some random run of good luck that might evaporate at any moment. Before the game, I had put a lot of time into scheduling conversations with prospective clients, consistently coaching others and getting coached myself. I pulled that same intentionality and focus into the game while actively learning from Dave and Gary. I took on every challenge and then some. All three of us were relentlessly committed to powerfully serving.

And I began to see that the consequences of fearless service are profound and reach way beyond the financial rewards. The impact is life-changing: prosperity at all levels.

GAME ON.

PART III: PRACTICING SERVICE

The problem is our inability or unwillingness to ACCEPT what we get and to work masterfully with that.

~ Chris Dorris

26

Mastery Milestones

If you could see behind the scenes of the "making of" you on your path, if you could read the script knowing who you would become, how you would feel (confident, peaceful, creative, alive and free!) and what you would create—you would be so energized and inspired that you would never stop. You would keep on the service path. You would be devoted to it.

From botched enrollment conversations and bungled sales communications to the days when you're weighed down by self-judgment—all of those experiences are cobblestones that pave your path to self-mastery.

But if you experience your efforts as a series of ongoing failures that confirm your worst fears, then you're bound to feel defeated and hopeless. You might even give up. So please slow down and really take this in. You've heard it before, but it bears repeating:

Failing is required. Your failures are your very own

mastery milestones in disguise. Without failure, there is no progress.

Look back over your life. School, sports, friendships, dating. Did you drop out of school if you received a D or even an F in a course? I certainly hope not. Did you see yourself as damaged goods, never to find love again after being dumped by your high school sweetheart? I doubt it. Did you remain friendless throughout life after your best friend stopped talking to you in middle school? Of course not!

Sure, you may have obsessed over these awkward and uncomfortable experiences, but you didn't take it as evidence you should stop. In fact, as you continued to grow, you saw these challenges as part of the game called life. And your responses to these events—whether you saw them as failures or successes—were significant stages in your development.

If your ego tells you (like mine told me) that because you're older and wiser now you won't have to make mistakes or get uncomfortable or take action when you don't know what the hell you're doing, your ego is wrong!

Professional coaches pass through multiple milestones to become proficient at client enrollment and coaching. Sometimes they even loop back to repeat one step or another. Learning is messy. It doesn't always fall in line and follow the perfectly laid out steps in a self-made plan or a self-help book.

But I have found that, over time, learning gets *easier*.

Once you really absorb the truth that 1) failing is learning, 2) learning is growth and 3) your personal growth is absolutely essential for your business's growth, then you will welcome the gift of your mastery milestones, whether they appear as failures or successes.

My own failures have been the keys to my growth, bringing me freedom and rewards like nothing else.

Permit me to share some of my favorites with you.

27

Recovering

I've screwed up a helluva lot of coaching conversations. You name it; I've done it.

- I've turned engaging social conversations into awkward offers for coaching.
- I've pushed prospective clients instead of slowing down and listening.
- I've sweated and stammered through initial fee conversations.
- I've missed opportunities to continue serving by avoiding renewal conversations with existing clients because I didn't want to appear needy or pushy.
- I've played "Coach-as-God" in sessions instead of helping someone uncover their own wisdom.

You have to engage in trial and error; there's no way

around it.

For me, the hard part wasn't the trial or the error; it was the self-judgment I heaped on afterwards and the nagging worry that "This time I've *really* done it! My reputation is ruined and no one will ever work with me again."

With the help of my coach, good colleagues and my own internal desire (the flame flickered low on numerous occasions, but it never fully went out), I didn't quit. I continued to practice and, with time, my facility for enrolling clients improved. But the most substantial spike in my enrollment numbers occurred when I learned the art of recovering: going back to a prospect (or client) and being candid, calling myself out, and apologizing if needed.

Recovering after rejection or failure was terrifying to me. Why would I purposely walk back into so much unpleasantness? It was like returning to the scene of a crime.

Yet return I did. Not once, but over and over. I cultivated the practice of doing the very thing I didn't want to do after I'd realized there was a more effective way of handling a conversation.

For example, when necessary I would go back to a prospect and admit I'd been rushing our conversation and trying to push my agenda, and I'd apologize. I'd offer a conversation "do-over" if they were willing, which would allow us to get back on track. Or if I felt like a client wasn't really getting what he needed in our work, I'd bring it up, telling him my concern and asking him how he felt about our progress—rather than keeping the concern to myself and hoping he wasn't disappointed that he'd hired me. Or if I had missed something during a session, I'd send an email offering a spot-coaching call so I could share what I had missed.

I found that I could always recover. Always.

What's more, learning to recover taught me humility that strengthened rather than weakened me. This act of "calling myself out" turned into a natural, loving thing to do for myself and for my clients. For me, it alleviated the old practice of judging myself after a conversation went wrong, and it allowed me to replace those negative thoughts with kind, true *action*. For my clients, my newly developed honesty and directness translated into much greater service.

How?

By opening up in humility and thoughtful reflection, I felt closer to my clients and prospects, and they to me. They trusted me more and were more inclined to be direct and truthful with me. Our coaching sessions were highly productive because we weren't protecting our egos, trying to please each other or hiding those things that really needed to be said and worked on together.

Recovering—ongoing acts of honesty, ownership

and a willingness to speak up without always having to get things exactly right—was turning me into a better servant-leader in my coaching and client enrollment.

Getting into action and recovering beat the hell out of stewing and blaming myself if I saw I could have handled a client enrollment conversation more effectively. It acknowledged my learning and moved me back into service.

Here's an example of how all this played out for me.

An experienced businesswoman wanted to discuss transitioning from her corporate job into her own consulting business. We had a couple of good conversations, during which she gained more clarity and started to outline her next steps. She asked me about the logistics of coaching, including my fee. When I shared all this information with her, she flat-out refused to work with me.

"I can't afford that! I'm sorry I took your time; I'd really love to work with you, but that's way outside my range."

Later, when I was running game film with my coach, I admitted that I would have said no to my offer, too.

"Why is that?" my coach asked.

"Because she doesn't yet know the value she can create through coaching."

"Do you really want to work with her?"

"Yes! She's super motivated and I could really help her get up to speed more quickly."

"Well if that's the case, go back and tell her why you would have said no, too, and if it makes sense, offer something else that will serve her. You've got nothing to lose."

So I emailed her, asking if she'd like to talk again because there was something important I wanted to share with her. She agreed, and during our next conversation I confided that I would not have accepted my offer either. It just didn't make good business sense. A look of surprise passed over her face.

I continued, "The reason it doesn't make sense is that you've never had coaching before and we've only talked a few times. You don't know what transformation is possible for you. You've never experienced ongoing conversations to help you find greater clarity, access your own wisdom and progress toward your goals with greater speed."

We continued to talk, and I ended up offering her a shorter engagement for a lesser fee. She accepted.

Now, I'm not recommending that you offer smaller engagements every time a prospective client tells you no. And definitely don't discount your fees.

What I *am* saying is that you can ask for a re-do. Don't miss opportunities to serve because you're

worrying over "what went wrong." Go back. Say what's true for you, and if there was a screw-up, *own it*. Straight and simple. No need to make yourself bad or wrong. You're simply learning. Recovering allows you back into relationship with the person, right where you need to be to continue to serve. Recovering replaces wallowing and worrying and wronging yourself. It gives you options to make things right. It puts you back in integrity, helps you feel good again and shows others they can do the same. And your prospects and clients can see that your number one priority is serving them—the basis of all trusted coaching relationships.

28

Drop that "Coaching" Thing

When most coaches first enter the world of professional coaching, they spend a lot of time trying to sell their services. They talk up their coaching and how it works, their certifications and their years of experience. There's a lot of explaining about the life transforming benefits of coaching.

In short, it's all about them and their coaching.

Well, isn't that the way it should be?

When I entered the coaching world I figured if I wanted clients I'd have to do the same. Get out there and push my coaching business in a professional way. I'd need a free-flowing pitch, an effortless way to weave the topic of coaching into any conversation. Once I mastered these sorts of skills, I'd be a natural at selling. The line would go out the door and around the block.

So I mastered my elevator pitch. I sent emails to prospects offering coaching sessions and letting them

Living Service ♥ 121

know that coaching is a game-changer and life always gets better with coaching. When they didn't respond, I'd "check back in" to see if they were ready for coaching. I knew that if I could just get them to experience the power of coaching, really *see* its value, then getting their yes would be easy.

That was not turning out to be the case.

One day, one of my coaches—Ron Wilder—suggested I stop it.

"Stop what?" I asked.

"You talk about coaching a lot. Not a good idea."

"I do?"

"Yeah," he said. "You're overly focused on communicating to people that you're a coach and that you provide coaching. Why don't you drop that 'coaching' thing?"

I was getting uncomfortable.

He continued: "We have nine months left in our work together. For the remainder of this time, eliminate the word 'coaching' from your vocabulary. Think of it as an experiment. When you talk to someone or send an email or a text, you can't type or even utter the word 'coaching.' Got it?"

I was quiet for a moment. Then: "Uh, well, sorta . . ."

"Here's what you don't get, Melissa. People don't buy coaching! They aren't interested in spending money on coaching, nor do they want to hear about your coaching career and how coaching can improve their lives. People only care about one thing."

I looked at him expectantly.

"Whether and how you can help them."

Finally it started to sink in. I had been a coach without a coach for years. When I finally hired my first coach, I was buying *help*—not coaching.

I needed someone to help me untangle the mental mess I had created that kept me stuck in fear, that kept me from living the life and building the business I wanted.

"Okay," I said, nodding. "But how am I going to communicate what I do and who I am?"

He smiled. "I'm sure you'll figure it out."

At least one of us was sure.

But, as Ron promised, I *did* figure it out. I felt my confusion start to lift . . . gradually. Instead of looking for people I could pitch, I listened to people I could help. I listened for problems and desires and I heard people telling me how they wanted their lives and relationships to improve. I began inviting people to talk further, to sit down in a professional capacity and have a conversation.

Who wouldn't want a kind, generous invitation to get clarity in their life versus a "session" to "come in and kick the coaching tires"?

Having found a way to move the focus off me and my coaching, I found that I was naturally serving.

One way this change came through was in my emails, which shifted from what they had typically been in the past:

```
Hi Shaun,
Let's get a time on the calendar and I
can tell you about the ways I work with
people and my success stories with my
clients. Then we can see if there's a
fit to work together and you can decide
if you want to continue. Either way,
you'll be glad you spent some time with
me! Let me know what date/time works
for you.
```

Or:

```
Hi Elise,
Good seeing you and your daughter
yesterday! She's really grown up! I
don't know if you're aware of this, but
I'm a coach now, and I work specifically
with parents to help them have better
relationships with their children. Your
relationship with your daughter is
amazing and I'd like to gift you a free
coaching session so you can experience
the power of coaching. That way you'll
have a better idea about my work in case
you ever have any friends or family
```

> members who need help, and you'll be more comfortable referring them to me. Let me know if you'd like the gift of a coaching hour. Anything I can do to serve!

But when I "dropped the coaching thing" my emails started looking more like this:

> Hey Ryan,
>
> I know you expressed real concern about your job and wanting to make a transition. If you'd like to talk, let's find a time so we can get you some relief as well as a good night's sleep. We can focus on anything that would provide you with some clarity around what's next for you. Let me know if you'd like to do that. I have next Tuesday open at 9 am.

Or:

> Hi Kimberly,
>
> If it would be useful, would you like to sit down and talk about what's happening with you and your husband? I hear your worry and frustration and I know this has been hard. We can focus on getting you clarity so things feel easier and more hopeful too. Let me know and we can set aside some time just for you.

People felt the difference with these emails because

the intention behind them had changed. It was no longer about me, my coaching, my track record. It wasn't about getting someone to want coaching or to give me referrals. It wasn't an email cloaked in service lingo to disguise that it's all about me. It was about *them*, their well-being, their world and a simple offer to help.

This is key: I was (and am) genuine in my desire to help. In shifting the focus off myself and my coaching in my emails, getting clients became *secondary* to helping the people I was reaching out to. I'm not going to lie and say that I couldn't care less if I ever got any clients. But my intention was first and foremost to serve, and this came through in my emails and in my conversations.

The response was overwhelmingly positive; people said yes to my offers.

By trying to get others to want "coaching," I unknowingly erected a barrier between us. Now, of course, this doesn't mean that I've completely stopped using the word "coaching." I still talk about it, but first I check my intention.

Am I pushing coaching? Is my focus on me and my coaching?

Or am I giving people what they really want? Is it about them?

Giving people what they really want is possible when you drop that "coaching" thing.

29

Money Commits

Things often went downhill when I came to the money part of a coaching proposal.

Even though I had practiced my delivery over and over—saying my fee out loud and trying to remain calm (or to at least appear casual)—my confidence frequently failed me. How, I wondered, would the prospect react to my fee.

Shocked? Offended? Would they object? Would they reject me?

There was one time when a prospect pulled out his calculator, figured out the hourly breakdown and then told me no.

Another time, I got up the courage to say my new, higher fee and, to my surprise, the prospect happily agreed! We were figuring out possible coaching dates and then she asked about a payment plan.

I said, "I'm open to it. What do you propose?"

She said, "How about three payments of $500?"

I was perplexed. Now, I'm not the greatest at math but even I knew something was off. "I'm not sure I understand," I said. "What do you think the fee is?"

She told me a sum that was thousands of dollars less. Right then and there I realized I had slipped up and had inadvertently dropped a zero.

I forced out a weak laugh. "I'm so sorry. I did say that. I misspoke." Then I told her the actual fee—and it was her turn to feel surprised! Of course, she made a graceful exit by telling me she'd think about. A kind way of declining my offer.

When a prospect says no to a coaching proposal, it often isn't about the fee (even if you screw it up). It's because they haven't yet seen the value of what your work together could create in their life. Things haven't changed enough for them after that first or second or even third conversation to merit an investment in coaching.

I know—through experience—the power of coaching, but the prospect often doesn't. So I learned to slow down, to spend more time with the client and on my enrollment conversations.

But the money part was still sticky, because I simply didn't understand the relationship of money to service.

Like many coaches, I saw service as the free stuff:

complimentary coaching sessions and unlimited resources like books, videos, audios, special quotes—anything that might be helpful. Service was everything up to the moment I asked to be paid.

Then it was all about *me*.

I was asking for your money, and this raised all sorts of questions inside me:

- Was I taking advantage of you?
- Was I making your life harder?
- Did I really care about you?
- And if you needed my help but couldn't afford it, wasn't I cold-hearted and selfish not to work with you?

Money only benefitted me, NOT you.

What I didn't realize at first was that I had plenty of personal evidence to the contrary.

I had invested thousands of dollars into my own development with my coach. That money committed me, pushed me to tap into a reserve of courage and take action that I wasn't able to take on my own. When I compared my experience of working with my coach with my experiences of receiving peer coaching for which no money changed hands, I saw the stark contrast.

At a certain point in my thinking around this issue of

Living Service ♥ 129

money and my clients, my own coach's words finally got through to me: "The highest form of service is a paid coaching relationship."

With my coach, I brought a higher level of consciousness to my sessions. I became the consummate student, willing to set aside my ego in order to learn. In other words, I was more open to transformation because, hell, I had paid for it!

I took any recommendation my coach made and agreed to test it out and report back on the outcomes. If our call was at 9:00 a.m., I was on time and prepared. After our calls I reviewed my notes. If I'd recorded our coaching calls, I listened to them again and again to draw out more nuggets.

Paying money shifted my internal state even before the coaching began. I wasn't committed to being right; I was committed to change.

Excuses were examined rather than clung to. I opened up to the possibility that the truths I had hung onto for the longest time were merely stories that could change on a dime.

I did learn from peer coaching, but the fact is that I wasn't as open, trusting or committed as when I paid for coaching. I unconsciously brought my ego to the conversations, either defending my actions to my peer coach or not really letting the coaching in. I got in my own way.

I recently offered a coaching session to a peer who happily accepted. A few days before our session she texted me, "Now isn't a good time. Can I use the session later?"

If she had paid for that session she wouldn't have cancelled. She would've maximized the opportunity. Essentially, she declined a gift worth hundreds of dollars because she saw it as "free" coaching. She never rescheduled.

And there's another perspective on this picture. I've learned that money not only commits the client, it commits the coach.

I see the difference in myself when interacting with a paid client. I bring a level of professionalism and elevated awareness to each session that just isn't as present when I'm simply helping someone out. I'm intentional in how I show up. I'm on time. Sessions don't get cancelled. Paid clients are a priority on my calendar.

Really understanding all this has changed the way I experience the process of proposing a paid coaching engagement to a prospect. Nowadays I look forward to it. I know the kind of transformation that awaits this prospect if they are willing to accept the highest form of service I can offer.

30

No Niche Necessary

I put off coaching in search of my people. I researched the hell out of my tribe. Visited places they frequented online and offline. Learned their lingo. Understood their pressing problems and deepest desires.

It was an anthropological endeavor.

I proudly told my coach about my research, but he wasn't overly impressed. Instead he asked about my results.

"How is client creation going?"

It wasn't. I had ZERO clients.

"So for the time being," he said, "why don't you forget about having a niche? Why don't you just help someone?"

It was hard to argue with common sense, but I made the effort anyway. "I may not be qualified," I whined. "I can't help everyone."

"Aren't you qualified to coach humans? Just offer

someone a conversation."

I guessed I was qualified to coach humans. I knew a lot about them. They had thinking problems . . . just like me.

The truth is that when I was real and honest with myself, I knew what was troubling me—and it had nothing to do with target markets. I was simply worried about being judged if I offered a conversation to help.

Was I being a nuisance?

Too pushy?

Creating an awkward situation?

I was far more comfortable researching and delaying instead of connecting with someone and possibly getting turned down. Recognizing this, I promised myself that I would stop hiding, courageously push aside my jittery nerves and begin.

I knew a number of parents who worried about their children; I could relate. In fact, parenting challenges had brought me to coaching. Fortified with the desire to help, I took all kinds of action, offering conversations to parents, speaking to PTO school groups, messaging neighbors with kids, writing for a local online paper . . . Soon I began coaching parents. They loved having someone to share their fears and frustrations with. Someone who really listened. Someone who helped them see their children with more loving, compassionate eyes.

I coached. And coached. And . . .

Suddenly it seemed I had a niche: parent coaching.

Then one thing led to another and I began talking with entrepreneurs, coaches, consultants, business owners, leaders . . . I wanted people in business to be successful, to increase growth and profitability, effectively communicate with their teams and become servant-leaders inside their companies and practices. I wanted them to love their work.

So I coached. And coached. And . . .

Suddenly it seemed I had another niche: business coaching.

Then I began helping people in their personal lives—rebuilding relationships with partners, family, friends and themselves. Clients began to see that they were prioritizing being right over feeling good, thinking they could only be happy if their loved ones changed first instead of changing their own perceptions. I even circled back to help parents create connected, respectful and kind relationships with their adult children.

I coached. And coached. And . . .

Niche number three: life coaching.

Lesson learned: a niche was never necessary. I just needed to begin.

31

Working Coach
vs.
Prosperous Coach

Be a working coach first; prosperity will follow.

Kamin Samuel

My income during my first few years as a professional coach was dismal. The math didn't lie: prosperity was a far-off dream if it meant breaking six figures.

I knew about the world of high-fee coaches who ran global coaching enterprises and utilized their unique talents to separate themselves from the pack, bringing in seven figures plus. Some had strong speaking businesses while others had well established online presences. Some were prolific, best-selling authors and others were shining extroverts who could light up a room and everyone in it.

Maybe I needed a bigger vision? Or maybe I had a

self-imposed "upper limit" issue around how much money I could create? Or maybe I had come too late to the professional coaching game?

Whatever was going on, I needed to find a faster way to prosperity so I took what I considered to be a more empowered, confident approach. I set higher fees, spoke highly of myself and my work, turned away people who weren't committed to a year-long investment in coaching and declined offers to speak for free.

My strategy was to act like a prosperous coach, "faking it until making it."

Soon, fake became the new fail.

Opportunities quickly dried up, people balked at my fees and I was back to asking myself the same old questions: Who do I talk to? Who will pay for my coaching? Will I ever succeed?

I was a broke "prosperous" coach.

I finally got real with myself and admitted where I was in my development. This brought me back to fundamentals. I returned to scheduling time to create clients, offering coaching conversations and slowing myself down to really serve. I could do that—and I determined I would *keep* doing that until I saw something else to do. No more short-cuts. No more excuse-making. No more hoping and wishing I'd win that high-fee client. No more acting like I was somewhere I wasn't.

I needed to forget about the monetary results and help people. I dialed it back, rolled up my sleeves and became a working coach.

Day in and day out.

Being a working coach built my confidence and paid the bills. Simply put, I could enroll clients at lower fees and be a paid, professional coach. I spoke pro bono to any group who would ask me, offering coaching conversations to my audiences, coaching more people and enrolling more clients. Over time, my fees increased as my coaching and enrollment got stronger.

As a working coach, I stopped comparing my efforts to my idea of what a prosperous coach should be. My dining room office was no longer evidence of my failure. Neither was the nominal fee I received for a speaking gig, nor the fact that sometimes it took three or four conversations before a prospect asked to work with me (unlike a "prosperous coach"—who I was certain enrolled high-fee clients after a thirty-minute call).

As a working coach, I took everything except 1) coaching, and 2) opportunities to coach more people right off my plate.

Out went my blogging and e-newsletters, my half-hearted efforts in the social media arena and an endless stream of networking events.

Anything that didn't light me up or feel like real service was eliminated.

If you love social media and connecting with people online, don't stop. If you love to write, do it! Get a kick out of being at the front of the room? Go speak. Be in the world helping people in your own unique way.

But for God's sake—be a working coach *first*!

Because if you don't become a working coach, you'll forever be racing down all the paths that *don't* lead to prosperity, including the path of pretending to be prosperous.

A woman who had launched her business about six months prior to contacting me was extremely frustrated that it still wasn't profitable. She had crafted a business plan, identified her target market, had a kickass logo and website, developed a comprehensive social media strategy including email blasts and posts, and she spent hours on the phone spreading the word about her exciting new profession. She even had a book in the works to enhance her status on the speaking circuit.

She supplemented these efforts with ongoing professional development, reading books and blogs, watching videos, listening to audios and consuming anything that would help build her business.

She had done everything to set herself up for success. Everything but being a working coach.

On our first call I asked her, "How do you think a coach creates a prosperous businesses?"

"Good question," she said. "I thought I knew, but it's clear I don't. I can see the final product—the prosperous coach with a multi-six-figure practice and lots of clients, successful and relaxed. I see the *before* picture and the *after* picture. But I don't know the in-between. The journey. I don't know how they got there!"

I shared what I'd learned.

"Those coaches first become working coaches by getting focused and dropping all distractions (the visioning, the preparing and the strategizing). They unsubscribe from mailing lists. They block off their mental exit ramps (careers or jobs they could go back to if this 'coaching thing' doesn't work out). They stop acting as if they have it all together, and they get help.

"They put their time into conversations and serving others. They become working coaches who serve, then become paid working coaches, who get better and better at their craft, creating extraordinary value and amazing transformation for their clients, day in and day out.

"Until one day they become prosperous coaches."

32

Fee Creation
vs.
Fee Confusion

I wanted to be paid well for my work. Certainly I was qualified; I had years of experience and I continued to invest in ongoing training and coaching as well. But I didn't feel confident when it came to selecting a fee, let alone saying it out loud. Maybe it was too high? Or too low? What would a high-fee coach charge? And who the f#%k do I think I am to charge that?!!

I allowed myself zero creativity when it came to establishing a fee. I was so concerned about people's responses. Would they balk? Burst out laughing? Flat out say "no"? Comment on how expensive I was and how other great coaches charged less?

How would I handle that?

On the flipside, maybe I'd say my fee and they'd happily pay it and tell me I was worth much more!

Either way it looked like I'd lose.

To deal with my confusion and uncertainty, I went in search of the "right" fee to charge, the industry standard. For me right meant safe. Safe from others' judgments, safe from making mistakes, safe from feeling bad—or worse, rejected. But my search didn't uncover any right fee. Every coach I spoke to had different packages and fees.

Some worked hourly, others charged by the result the prospect wanted to create, and still others on a monthly or annual basis.

Eventually I discovered there is no right fee; it doesn't exist. Like everything else it's purely creative. So I had to get creative, which as in so many things meant being willing to start somewhere.

Anywhere!

In the beginning, the best piece of advice I ever received regarding fees was this: charge a fee for which

- if the prospect says yes, I'm excited to work with them
- if the prospect says no, I'm happy to part ways.

But do what feels right for *you*. Listen to yourself. Charge a fee that inspires you, or one that puts food on the table. Charge a fee that you know people will say yes to, or charge one that's a stretch. It doesn't matter.

Just set a fee and begin. You can always revisit it later.

In my own case, I just picked a number. One I wouldn't choke on while saying it out loud. One that I, myself, would pay.

Then I took the next—dreaded—step: I tested it out. And I kept at it, offering coaching, helping people, saying my fee until it felt natural. Over time, as my skills strengthened, my fees increased. They do for every coach.

Recently, I was coaching a group of coaches who shared their diverse opinions on what fee to charge, highlighting their own inner wisdom about what was right for them in that moment. Some of their responses:

- I charge a higher fee so I can fully serve my existing clients. Otherwise I get overloaded with clients and don't have time to really make a difference.
- I just need to fill my practice. I charge a smaller fee so it's easy for people to work with me. Right now, I just need to be a paid coach.
- I've been holding out for a high fee but I'm not enrolling clients. I have monthly expenses I

need to meet, so I'm going to scale back my fee.
- I like my fees. I'm sticking with what feels good.

Each of these coaches knows that their approach works for them today, and they can build from there, adjusting as desired. All of these coaches have embraced the freedom of creating their own fee, testing it out, evaluating it and, if necessary, changing it to fit their needs and their ability to serve their clients.

You can do the same.

33

It Isn't a YES

Early on in my coaching career, I offered a session to a female entrepreneur who seemed like the perfect prospect: dynamic, creative and enthusiastic. We had a powerful session, brainstorming initial steps she could take to eliminate busy work that kept her from doing what she needed to do to grow her business. By the end of our conversation she wanted to continue coaching.

So far so good. I was successfully executing my enrollment process checklist:

- Invite someone to a conversation. Check.
- Have a powerful coaching session and make a difference. Check.
- Have my proposal ready prior to the conversation rather than make up something on the fly. Check.
- Make the offer. Check.

I comfortably explained the details to her, including the fee, which was payable in advance. She said YES! We scheduled her first session.

I followed up with some additional resources. Check.

I had arrived!

I had figured out how to enroll a client. And not just any client, but a high-fee one. And I did it with ease and grace and simplicity. I felt masterful.

I shared the good news with my husband, close friends and colleagues, and I even called my mother! I was ecstatic. Years of diligently offering conversations to prospects, coaching them, running game film, uncovering what I could do differently and then *repeating* this cycle . . . and *finally* it was over! Officially OVER! I was relieved and proud that I had stayed the course. I felt I was stepping into freedom.

I thought: *So this is how a prosperous coach feels.*

On the designated day of her kickoff session, I woke up ready to serve. I felt relaxed and excited to bring my best to whatever would unfold.

The appointed hour came . . .

And then it went.

No text, email or call.

No client.

I called her office and was told she was out. I left my name and number. Then I sent a text. No response.

What had gone wrong?

I had done everything by the book!

My initial response? Anger. I was mad as hell at this rude, insensitive person. But the burn of anger soon dissolved into embarrassment as I recalled all the people I had "humbly" bragged to. And I felt confused, too, remembering how smoothly the whole enrollment process had gone. I had gotten through the hard part, hadn't I? Having the prospect ask to work with me. Getting the YES. Putting the date on the calendar. It should have played out perfectly!

But it didn't.

It unraveled.

Self-righteous indignation was a tempting response, but I now knew better. I had seen again and again how nothing good ever comes out of being a righteous victim. I wouldn't win anything by holding a grudge close to my heart or creating a hardship story to share with friends and family.

I also knew that I'd be destined to repeat whatever mistake I'd made if I didn't take the wiser route by staying open and reflecting on my part in this deal gone south.

Had I really helped her? Or had I given her just enough so she'd inquire about working with me? Had she experienced an internal change, really seen something at a deeper level that would inspire her to invest in coaching? Or had I simply impressed her with information and a confident presence? Was hers a strong yes or was I just too eager to close the deal?

Gradually, it all became clear.

I'd been so focused on getting a client that I'd moved too quickly. I had run through a *process* perfectly, but come up empty-handed. I'd wanted a standard operating procedure for client creation. Give me the formula and I'll apply it for the win!

Of course, it turns out there is no "by-the-book," no magical questions or guaranteed "right" steps. If there were, I would have had a new client and money in my bank.

Since that experience, I now see that each new prospect requires me to simply go where I think it will best serve that individual. Often it feels counterintuitive, the last place I'd venture when trying to "get" a client, but then I remind myself that I am not here to "get." I'm here to serve.

If I had been unattached to enrolling this entrepreneur, I would have slowed down after she said yes and asked:

"Does this sound exciting? Are you ready to do this? Is there anything else we need to discuss before we proceed?"

I would have tested her yes—not as another step in my enrollment process but because *I really wanted to know*.

To see if yes really meant yes.

My coach had been telling me that a standardized enrollment process didn't exist. That applying a sales process to a person never works. I now believed him. The only thing that creates a client is when that person experiences a shift of perspective. They see something new. They connect with their inner knowing. And they understand that our work together will put them on the path to achieving what they desire.

Transformative service creates the yes.

The yes you can count on.

The yes spoken by a true, committed client who's ready for more.

34

Sisyphus System

Here I was, once again, with no new prospects on the horizon. How many times had I been here before, battling an inconsistent flow of income, bouncing back and forth between times of plenty (when I had a full roster of clients) and periods of scarcity (when clients had completed their coaching engagements with me)? Five or six at least.

The cycle was getting old, and I was burning out—especially considering how much time I had put into learning and practicing service.

I felt like the mythological king, Sisyphus, damned for his arrogance and multiple misdeeds to eternally roll a massive boulder up a hill—only to have it reach the top and watch it roll back down again. This is how I felt every time clients completed with me—it was time to run back down the hill and begin the enrollment process once again.

But heading back to the top was tough; I just couldn't get any momentum.

Where was that effortless, natural flux of incoming clients that was supposed to happen once I'd mastered enrollment? Why, instead, was I experiencing an erratic flow of clients and wondering if I could ever create and sustain a viable business?

Everyone has a system for client creation, my coach preached. Even those coaches who say they don't; they have one. They just haven't looked close enough. If you don't like your results, change your system!

If you want to discover your own system, start by asking yourself these questions, and write down your answers:

- How does my system operate?
- What works?
- What hasn't been working?
- What do I like about it?
- What do I tolerate?
- What's missing?
- Is there anything surprising about my system?
- Do I know someone with a system I really like? If so, what are they doing?
- (And for fun) What name would I give my system?

Please slow down and take this in.

This isn't an evaluation of you. It's an assessment of your client acquisition system. Nothing personal. Notice that there aren't any questions like "Where did I go wrong?" or "How (and why) did I fail, once again?" or "What kind of loser am I that I'm still struggling with getting clients?"

Don't go there. This is an objective evaluation. A simple diagnostic test.

These questions don't comprise a superficial checklist to tick through. Take time to reflect upon them. In doing so you'll be assessing the functionality of your system and its ability to create the results you say you want. Answer these questions honestly and thoughtfully, especially the ones that bring up uncomfortable responses. There's real value in your answers. Monetary value.

If you aren't getting the results you want, that means there's a breakdown in your system and you need to do what all profitable businesses do—redesign your system.

My answers to these questions uncovered the inner workings (and bugs) of what I half-jokingly named my "Sisyphus System."

Here's how it worked:

I would clear the decks (both mentally and on my calendar), fully focusing on client creation through scheduling enrollment conversations with prospective clients until my days were filled. I kept this up, sometimes offering numerous sessions to one person, until I had a full client roster.

Then I would stop.

The boulder was up the hill. I had an active schedule, a little time to relax and money in the bank. The coaching was zinging along until, at some point, I'd start to wonder, "Hmmm, when are clients going to complete?"

Reviewing my list, I'd realize with horror that the boulder had begun to roll back down the hill!

Suddenly awake to this state of affairs, I'd frantically

get back into client-creation mode and try to stave off the stress and strain of a financial gap. During one epic round of panic, I had six year-long clients completing within a few months of each other, requiring a four-month period of client enrollment calls until my schedule was full once again.

That round was the last straw.

It was now crystal clear where my Sisyphus System broke down.

The question was: why did I stop talking to prospective clients when I had a full client roster?

Because I was operating under a fundamental misunderstanding, one that I see many coaches falling prey to. There's this idea that at some point, business just naturally flows in; people line up to work with you. I had seen other prosperous coaches being specifically sought out and contacted just out of the blue by people wanting to be their apprentices or sign up for their programs and be willing to pay high fees for the privilege. All because they had heard that the coach was good. For these coaches, it appeared that paid clients just "happened."

This led me to conclude that once I got that boulder up the hill I could sit back like those other seasoned coaches and wait for clients. Then I could do what I really loved, and nothing else: coach.

Wrong!

Unlike me, those other prosperous coaches had been in this coaching business for years. They had built up sweat equity. They had books, podcasts, live events, online programs and great reputations. And as I looked even more closely, I could see that clients weren't being created out of thin air! These coaches had well-oiled systems that looked effortless and, from afar, non-existent. But these systems had in fact evolved over time, and they were very real.

My system would evolve, too, as long as I stayed conscious of it.

It was naïve of me to believe that I'd reach a point where client acquisition wouldn't require my time or focus. That was where I stopped treating my business like a business.

Businesses can't exist without sales.

I remember hearing years ago from my coach, Steve, that the difference between successful coaches and struggling ones was that the former LOVED sales. If you hated sales or merely tolerated it, or even if you liked it, you'd feel stress every time a client completed. You had to learn to love it.

And so another piece of the puzzle fell into place for me.

I was earning my living based on 100 percent commissions, yet my sales department (yours truly) worked only when clients completed. And I was waiting to "make it" to the point at which I wouldn't have to sell anymore. That's not how business works!

My system required a simple, yet paradoxical fix: 1) keep the sales department doors open regardless of a full client roster and 2) develop a LOVE of sales by serving powerfully, with no attachment to getting any clients.

With this new system, my business started working for me. I stayed in ongoing conversations with prospective clients, seeing how I could help and making a difference in those conversations. Some signed on, and others didn't.

That effortless, natural flux of incoming clients came as a result of a simple, functional system that served me, my clients and my business.

Stay conscious of your current system, revisiting it from time to time to ensure it supports the kind of coaching business that you'd love to create.

35

Slowing Down to Powerfully Serve

My coach counsels calmly, kindly, "Relax. Go for a walk to settle your mind."

He reminds me to slow down.

At first I don't think he understands. I'm not into slowing down. I need to clear this up with him.

"See, Steve, I came to this coaching career later in life, so I need to speed up and get to where I'm headed. I don't have time for playing around."

I was tired of slow and steady. So I would double down and ask all kinds of questions about client enrollment:

How do I start a conversation?

When do I propose?

What kind of packages should I offer?

Was I charging enough? Too much?

Often, he'd answer my questions with another question or three, redirecting me: "Are you open to

Living Service ♥ 157

slowing this down? What would really help this person?"

There it was again: slowing down.

For me, slowing down wasn't a good thing. It meant checking out, caring less about growing my business, distracting myself or taking extended naps. But whenever I tried to speed up, Steve would caution me to slow down.

Then, finally, I understood. He wasn't asking me to decelerate or halt my progress. He wasn't even remotely suggesting I become purposeless, listless or pathetic.

He was referring to my thinking. He wanted me to slow *that* down. My low-grade, hyped-up thinking was getting in my way of serving others.

And I had *a lot* of it, that kind of thinking—most of which I took very seriously.

- I can't offer coaching to that person; she told me she's broke!
- Who am I to coach people inside corporate? I know nothing about that world!
- I've got to impress this person with all I know or otherwise they won't hire me!

Were any of these thoughts true? Did they open up new opportunities or have me falling down the rabbit hole? Did they uplift and inspire me or make me feel incompetent and incapable?

In truth, most of my thinking was just negative internal babel. Mental noise pollution. And it had me missing opportunities to serve.

For example, I might:

- Have a chance to offer a proposal that would really serve a prospect but hold back because I didn't want to hear NO.
- Rush an enrollment conversation because my thinking had convinced me that I had to convert a prospect into a client in one session (with the end result that the prospect would go away to think about it.)
- Frantically search for my "ideal" client but be blind to the neighbor or past colleague or good friend who could use my help.
- Turn on the charm so I could get something in return—a referral or a testimonial or a client—instead of just being present to serve.
- Resist scheduling coaching conversations because I was living in the fragile kingdom—that land of insecure thinking and self-deprecatory remarks into which I dropped at a moment's notice.

When I became so enmeshed in my thinking, I had problems and issues and all kinds of things to figure out, which led to more problems and issues and . . .

What stopped this tsunami of revved up, fear-based thinking?

Slowing down. Hitting the pause button.

Sometimes it was clearing my mind with a walk. I'd head to the nearby park and take in all the activity. Parents playing with their children or people walking their dogs or kids playing soccer. I was in another world, *not* the one in my head that was crowded with churned up stress and worry.

I began to enjoy the moment. I lost sight of myself in a good way. It reminded me of how I felt when I was a kid. Nothing on my mind. Just being.

In those moments, I didn't have problems plaguing me. I had an internal peace, a good, easy feeling that always brought me a new outlook.

Sometimes hitting the pause button happened when I asked myself a simple question:

What would truly serve this person?

Instead of answering this with my analytical mind, I'd once again go to that quiet space inside and reflect about the prospect or client. I'd get new ideas bubbling up from wisdom rather than stale, old ones spewed out by my mental chatter.

Or sometimes I glimpsed that my "problems" were just habitual thoughts passing by, coming and going no matter how hard I tried to control them, ignore them, or change them. Just seeing the truth of this relaxed me and reminded me that pure service comes from the love and peace accessible just beyond the cloud of my confused, jumbled thinking.

Slowing down means stepping out of my internal, thought-created world and into the world of powerful service.

36

The Service Equation

"So, it sounds okay, right? What do you see?"

I had crafted a renewal proposal for an existing client that just didn't feel right, and my dear friend and master coach, Sherry Welsh, had agreed to provide feedback on the logistics.

"Yes, it sounds fine," she said. "Yet you don't seem excited by your offer. Why is that?"

She had a point. I felt uninspired. Flat. Blah. A bit grouchy.

She continued, "How do you expect anyone to say 'yes' to what you're offering if you're unenthused?"

Another good point. Then she made a third:

"If it doesn't serve you, it won't serve your client. You need to be a part of the equation. So what would be *fun* for you to offer? Go with that!"

This was breaking news to me. There was actually some kind of "service equation"? Service wasn't just for my client?

Relief and joy washed over me. I'd evolved an extremely rigid definition of service that only considered my prospect's needs. I felt like I'd screwed up the service idea when I first started coaching, so it was vital to always and only serve the prospect—and certainly not ask what would serve *me*.

Now I felt giddy even considering that question.

With Sherry's prompt an idea bubbled up about what I really wanted to offer my client. The words rushed out:

"Instead of just offering more business coaching, I could offer to help her address the ongoing dissatisfaction she feels with her spouse and daughter. They aren't living up to her expectations and she thinks they're the source of her disappointment. They aren't—but she has yet to see that her emotional experience comes from her thinking, and if she wanted to, she could feel good regardless of their behavior." I summed up my monologue with, "So we'd focus on her *whole life* getting better!"

In that moment I saw that service really isn't a one-sided proposition. When I ask myself what would serve me *in addition* to my client, it opens the door to me bringing my own feelings of curiosity, excitement and adventure into the equation.

As coaches, we often leave ourselves out of the equation. When we do, a numbing dullness seeps in and blocks our creative impulses. There are many ways for a coach NOT to serve himself (and the client), including chasing money, pleasing prospects and too much focus on closing clients. I did all these things, but the real issue that kept me out of the equation was my perfectionistic mindset of trying to get it *right*.

The imperative to "get it right!" was always running in the background. The problem is that it was based on a made-up standard that I used to judge my actions. So instead of joyful anticipation of designing an upcoming coaching proposal, I'd obsess over whether it was "right," meaning that it would get my prospect to say yes. Or I'd play it safe and not tell my client what I really

thought, afraid that I'd get it wrong and they'd wonder, *Why the hell did I hire her?* I obsessed about setting the "right" fee, asking the "right" questions, conducting enrollment conversations the "right" way.

I put myself in a mental and emotional straightjacket with this crazy "right" pursuit.

No wonder I wasn't enjoying myself!

Chained to this strict definition of service, I allowed myself no access to my own creativity, my accumulation of knowledge and insight and my particular brand of humor and hard-headed persistence. All the things that would allow me to powerfully serve were inaccessible by my quest for getting it "right."

If service really was an equation, then in order to be a part of it, I had to be willing to get it WRONG. Make a mess of it.

So I went for it. REPEATEDLY.

As the pressure of perfectionism began to fade, something new and liberating began to happen. I became more human. I discovered I could do that perfectly. I started noticing I was less serious and more relatable. Less right and more open. And my willingness to be wrong gave my clients permission to be human, too.

We all started to breathe easier.

And that's only possible when you—the coach—are an integral part of the service equation.

All our philosophy is as dry as dust if it is
not immediately translated into
some act of living service.

~ Mahatma Gandhi

37

Service Clarity

What does "service" mean to you?

I've explored the idea of service throughout this book, but the truth is that every coach comes to the service path with a different understanding of the concept. I've heard so many coaches say, "Believe me, I know how to serve!" and then stand by surprised as they race past service into the "how-to's" and occasionally manipulative techniques of client creation.

So I suggest doing yourself (and your clients) a favor. Slow down. Get clear about what service means to you. Spend some time fleshing it out. Then ask yourself: *Do I like my definition of service? Why or why not? What do I see are the upsides and downsides of building a business through service? Have I ever experienced profound service from someone else? What was that like? How did I feel? What happened?* Uncovering your idea of—and relationship to—service can clear up misconceptions and, if necessary, help you create a new definition that resonates more with what you want to create for yourself and your clients.

A few years back, I ran a group for coaches who weren't getting much traction in growing their practices. They all believed in serving others, knowing that the work they did was life-changing. What they *didn't* know, however, was how "serving" a prospect could lead to a paid coaching relationship.

One coach defined service as giving away her coaching for free and then hoping the universe would send her a client because she had done a good deed. She had this "The-Universe-Has-Got-My-Back" system operating for years, but it was producing only a trickle of clients.

Another coach (of parents) knew her coaching was of great service to her clients, but in her experience they just wouldn't pay for it. They'd fork over unlimited funds for sports camps, international travel, education, etc., for their children—but investing in coaching so they could get better at lovingly guiding their kids? Uh-uh. (By the way, this was her money-fear story projected onto her prospects, which she's since moved beyond.) But because she felt her work was important, she decided she should just keep doing it free of charge. She'd tell herself, "It's not about the money. It's about me being able to help parents. Besides, I'm in a position where I can afford to help people for free." But her good feelings of giving back were often punctuated with twinges of resentment. There was no service being delivered because, in the end, prospective clients viewed her as a generous, wise person and NOT a professional coach.

Still another coach thought that service meant pleasing her prospects and clients. She'd turn on her charm and friendliness, exuding warmth and interest. Service for this coach meant having long talks with her prospects, engaging in deep listening, creating a safe space and really getting to know them. There was lots of texting back and forth whenever her "friends" wanted to share or when they needed free "advice"—which they LOVED! And she was puzzled that all this service didn't lead to paid clients. Couldn't they see she could help them?

My question to this group was: Why do so many coaches think that serving others means free coaching?

One reason, I think, is that service in our society is often equated with unpaid, volunteer work where we give lavishly of our time and are rewarded with feelings of love, abundance and connection. That's our remuneration. Although this altruistic mindset is beautiful and generous, in the world of running a coaching business it's untenable. Thriving businesses have one thing in common: profit. Otherwise, you won't be able to keep the doors open. As speaker, author and master coach Jason Goldberg astutely points out, "People who see service as 'give, give, give, give, give' . . . eventually give up!"

38

Service Is Creative

One client of mine struggled with his own definition of service. For him, service meant 24/7, open-hearted giving to the point of exhaustion—especially for those who couldn't afford it. His service was all about self-sacrifice, but he was burning the candle at both ends. Our coaching focused on blending his kind, service-oriented heart (and wicked sense of humor) with taking care of his own needs. In order to powerfully serve others, he needed R&R—rest and remuneration—otherwise he wouldn't be able to keep on coaching.

He needed to see that an exchange of money for his coaching served him and his clients. His clients' financial investment in coaching committed them to creating change. And for his part, not only did he commit himself to serving his client when compensated, he was also able to pay his bills and stay in business doing what he loved to do—transforming lives! As his understanding of service grew, so did the power and impact of his coaching and his income.

Then he took on a business client who proposed a guaranteed monthly income in exchange for coaching some of its leaders. Previously, he would have jumped at this offer, seeing it as a real win! A guaranteed monthly income? Who would say no to that?

He did. When he reflected on the proposal, something felt off. He saw that a guaranteed monthly fee wouldn't serve him or his client. It represented a different kind of commitment that he felt would not benefit him at this stage of his business. It would take him out of the game of client creation; he'd just be sitting back and having new clients funneled his way.

So he came up with a new idea. A new fee structure whereby he would be responsible for enrolling new clients inside the company. There would be no guaranteed income. He would be compensated for what he had created through service. As he negotiated this new deal with the executive assigned to the project, he explained that it wasn't in their best interest to provide a guaranteed monthly fee. That his proposal would allow both coach and client to engage a deeper level of personal commitment and investment in the coaching process.

Such a high level of service! And in this case it paid

off instantly: he enrolled the executive assigned to negotiate a guaranteed monthly rate.

Your best service occurs when you're doing your work as a fully engaged, paid professional. When you keep that in mind as your ultimate service, you won't be inclined to over-give or inappropriately share your skills. It's not a question of not helping; it's about both parties being fully committed when you *do* help.

Most coaches don't realize that their misunderstandings about service are blocking their flow of incoming clients and money. Confused, they either look outside themselves to explain their failure to make money, or they focus inward, questioning their abilities and desires. But usually the only problem is their working definition of service.

If you would like to improve your own understanding of and relationship to service, I offer you these thoughts:

- Get clear about what service means to you.
- Ask successful coaches who are further down this path what service means to them. Ask for examples and stories they can share. I guarantee that you'll see something in it for you!
- Be open to your understanding of service continuing to evolve. Through the ongoing

> practice of coaching others and running game film on your interactions, you'll see where your definition of service needs to be upgraded and strengthened. Take it on and test it out!

If service feels weak or shaky or there are aspects of it that still feel like a struggle, find a successful coach to work with you on it. Get help to grow *the attitude of service* inside of you so you can conduct powerful enrollment conversations and help people experience shifts even before they hire you. This keeps you confident and relaxed when it's time to walk a new client through the logistics of payment and scheduling their first few sessions. You will also learn when to stop serving someone who is simply not ready to create change and invest in coaching.

You will probably find—as I have—that as you continue your journey, service expands beyond the borders of business and coaching and unfolds in all areas of your life. You will clearly see that service isn't about "pleasing" or "giving advice" or being at the beck and call of friends and acquaintances when they need to unload. Service is about helping people by being present with them in a way that transforms their life—and your own.

39

Stay on the Path

I called this book *Living Service* because service has become my way of life.

I mentioned that early on in my journey I saw my coach, Steve Chandler, embodying the principle of service in every area of his life. But I never saw it as a possibility for myself. Nor did I really even understand what that would mean at that early stage.

Back then I could never have imagined the ups and downs and twists and turns ahead of me. I couldn't have seen how the fundamentals of what I needed to know were so counterintuitive to what I thought would bring me prosperity—including the kind of prosperity that has nothing to do with money. There were times when I felt like I was on top of my game and other times when I wondered why I persisted.

But I stayed on the path, even though I had no idea this "service thing" that I thought was supposed to "get" me clients would also reward me with a whole new world.

A whole new ME!

Indulge me for a moment as I share where I'm at now, even as I continue on my journey, because I fully believe—no, I *know*—that the same is entirely possible for all of us.

I've already explained that my initial reaction to service was resistance. When I hired Steve, I wasn't interested in transformation. The relationship was supposed to be purely transactional. I wanted to buy his secret for client acquisition.

I discovered that it wasn't for sale; it was something I'd have to learn.

So I tried to learn by asking how-to questions, by isolating a strategy or script that would lead directly to effectively closing clients. Did I have the right words? Was I serving the right way? I was "doing" service, to a degree, but it was a means to an end—getting clients. Playing the service game turned the idea of service upside-down and got me out of my head. With less focus on *me*, my ability to serve skyrocketed and so did my income.

And gradually I realized that a major shift had occurred within me. *Instead of* doing *service to snag a client, I was* being *service by coming from a place of caring and concern for another human being.*

At that point the question "How can I help?" didn't come with a hidden agenda of getting a paid client. It came with a sincere desire to make a difference.

Being service was the result of an internal reboot that led to a total upgrade.

40

Serving Loved Ones

The next upshift in service occurred when I realized I had compartmentalized my life, keeping service just for the professional side. There were two Melissas. One who showed up big-hearted and service-oriented as a coach to her clients, prospects and colleagues, and the other one who loved her family and friends but who habitually operated from a lower level of consciousness. A kind of "checked-out" approach to my personal life. I was so overly consumed with my own aspirations that I left little time for my personal relationships. For example, I kept my head deep in my own work when my husband came home, giving a half wave or half listening when he wanted to talk. As for how I saw myself, I had a continual stream of low-grade self-criticism running in the background which made it hard for me to be relaxed and loving of myself. And whereas I had all the patience in the world with a client to work through a problem, I was

Living Service ♥ 179

far less patient with myself and my family.

Why was that?

Did I think I wouldn't able to maintain the same level of focus and engagement in my personal relationships as I did in my professional ones? Or maybe I'd run out of energy and find myself depleted and exhausted from over-loving? Was I operating on the assumption that there was a limited supply of caring and connection that was all used up on the job?

What if I merged my two selves so that service was integral to my whole life? Not because I was supposed to, but because I knew how good I felt being that way with clients. What would it be like to be even five percent more loving and open in my personal life, as my coach suggested? I decided to try.

Coming from love, I was more thoughtful. For example, I began calling my husband during the day just to connect and hear how he was doing. Or, when my adult daughter called, I practiced a new way of loving her by listening without providing advice. Often the conversations would end with her texting me, "Thank you for listening to me! I'm so lucky!" Or I'd call my mom at the end of the day to catch up. I wanted her to know I was thinking of her.

In personal conversations, I noticed I preferred a loving connection over being right. I kept myself more open to someone else's viewpoint rather than arguing a contrary position. In situations which I noticed I was trying to control, I'd wonder: Is there really anything to fear? Really? What if I loosened my grip? Or what if I followed through on my word, doing what I said I'd do, rather than making excuses or blaming someone or something else?

What if I just got over the story that "I'm always the one who is putting in the effort?" And along with that—drop the mental scorecard!

Did I do this ALL perfectly? No. Perfection wasn't the goal—self-awareness, intentionality and being loving were.

41

Serving Yourself

All of this focus on living—and loving—service for my clients, family and friends transformed my life. So I asked, what if I focused on being five percent more loving of myself?

I got back into exercise, committing to consistent training which I've built upon over the years. The benefits of increased strength, flexibility and energy, endorphins flowing and me glowing, has improved all areas of my life, including my coaching.

When I was feeling negative or low, I engaged less and less in self-criticism, realizing it was just habitual thought I didn't need to take seriously. Over time, my tolerance for these negative narratives diminished. Five percent more loving in these instances meant being five percent kinder to myself. The need for perfection was replaced with compassion and even humor, which naturally extended to others. I dropped more and more of the "shoulds" I held for myself and others, allowing my own wants and others' expressions to naturally come through rather than judging them and thinking they should be different, as I had done in the past. Again, none of this is done perfectly because I'm human. I still feel judgmental or irritated or hurt. But I catch it sooner because I'm less invested in honoring old stories that don't serve me and I'm more open to loving and learning.

In a nutshell, my relationships deepened, my mood stayed higher, and I took better care of myself and those I loved. I was no longer turning service on and off. On for work. Off for life. On for clients. Off for family, friends and myself. And the more I brought service into my whole life, the easier it was to help my clients because I was coaching what I lived.

Prosperity goes way beyond financial rewards. It's being engaged in an intentionally created whole life of experiences, connections and moments that come from living service.

42

Keep Upgrading Your Service

As you grow and expand so will your level of service. One way to stay conscious of this is to continue to reflect on questions like the ones I share below. I ask these of myself all the time, and often of my clients. I've shared some of my own thoughts and answers about them, but you and your clients will also have your own. The beauty of these questions is that they'll prompt insights that open up whole new areas of the self for exploration.

What would help?

I love the simplicity of this question because it shifts me into the other person's world. Helping as a coach isn't identifying someone's "flaws" and then fixing them. No one needs (or wants) to be fixed. Helping someone is exposing them to new possibilities that they may never have considered before. It's helping them access their own wisdom and answers. And the most profound way to help is by receiving ongoing coaching from your own coach in all areas of your life. You can't ask others to do what you haven't been willing to do yourself. Your continuous evolution of waking up and growing up will transform you into an extraordinary coach who powerfully serves.

What would serve?

Illuminating truth—with a generosity of spirit for someone's highest good—is the ultimate service. For example, a friend and colleague of mine was feeling shaky about her coaching. What would serve her? A coaching session so that she might access her own inner knowing rather than just hearing quick advice on the fly from me. Or when a client is feeling self-critical and uncertain, slowing him down to reflect on what's really true versus the fiction he's spinning.

What would inspire?

Why not ask your client? They know what inspires them. And, if they don't, your question will give them an opportunity to find out. And when you ask *yourself* this question—for instance, when you're designing a proposal or a program—it helps you bring inspired creativity to your work, which in turns serves you and your clients.

What would love do?

This is one of my personal favorites. I first heard this question from master coach, Lori Cash Richards. This question moves me out of my typical, small thinking and opens me up to a stronger inner knowing, a place of compassion and love where the answer isn't one size fits all—it's original and tailor-made for each client. It also helps me in challenging situations, lifting me up from negative, victim-like thinking. "What would love do?" Almost immediately the answers come to me. Love can be direct and honest. It can jolt someone awake with a powerful question. Or it can set boundaries in a way that truly serves someone. Love always delivers.

What would lift someone up?

For starters: reflecting back to someone what I see in them. Their tenacity, kindness and openness to learning. Their willingness to test out new ideas. I want to stand for them especially when they aren't standing for themselves. I can even invite them to look back at what's changed for them over the time we've worked together. Often we fail to see the growth that we've created because we're so focused on what's next.

Look back and see the growth! It's guaranteed to lift you up.

What would wake someone up?

The truth, delivered in any way that it can be heard. Like when my coach asked me, "When are you going to stop living like you're never going to die?" That question really lit a fire under my you-know-what, having me commit to consciously creating my life rather than being a victim of my "reality" of life.

Or sharing a personal story with a client—in which a new insight changed my view—allows a client to be open to that possibility too.

Or telling someone I don't buy their story about why they can't have what they want, or how something outside of them is making their life hard.

What would make a difference?

This may sound paradoxical, but sometimes the perfect response to this question is to let someone know they don't *have* to change. At all! There's nothing wrong with who they are, what they do and what they want. Speaking this truth allows someone to change if they want to. It's their call. Sometimes removing the demand to change—whether it's coming from the client or someone else—actually inspires the change. Another way of looking at this is to not make something wrong as a prompt to change it. When we are at peace with ourselves, we can still want to operate differently.

In fact, change is easier when we do.

43

Service Becomes Your Life

Last year my dad passed on. He had suffered a series of strokes several years before, leaving my mom responsible for his medical care. As he neared the end of his life my mom had some tough decisions to make. Really she had the ultimate decision to make: whether or not to take my dad off life support.

At a different time in my life—before living service—I would have thought that I knew best about how to handle these end-of-life decisions. It amazes me to think that I could have been so arrogant, but I would have believed I was being practical, taking charge, doing the "right" thing. I would have let her know what I thought was best and then tried to direct her there.

Now, as I sat with my mom and her indecision, my understanding of service was right there with me. I knew I didn't know what was best for her or for my dad.

We were sitting in the hospital cafeteria together.

"Mom," I asked her, "how can I help?"

"There's nothing," she said quietly. "I thought I'd be able to make myself let him go now. But I still don't want to . . ." Her voice trailed off.

Over the last few days as my dad's condition had worsened, I had been dealing with my own emotional upset, but in this moment with a quiet mind, love rose to the surface.

"No need to force yourself, Mom," I said simply. "When you're ready, you'll know."

And she *did* know. For the rest of the day she let herself *be* so she could just sit with my dad again and love him. The next day my mom, my sister and I were all there as she let him go. For now.

When we embrace service we hold space for inner wisdom to come through. We welcome the moments of *not-knowing* in life, because these are the quiet, open spaces where understanding and love rush in.

We strengthen our ability to hold discomfort and acknowledge it, rather than deflecting it or letting it take us down. Service strengthens *who we really are*, not who we think we should be.

Living service is like a crazy feedback loop of loving kindness. The more we practice it, the more we see it moving through our personal lives to our professional ones and back and forth and over and under and everywhere in between.

44

You're Right Where You Need to Be

Wherever you are on the service path is exactly where you need to be.

It doesn't matter where your colleague is or where your coach is or where someone you follow on social media is.

It doesn't matter that you thought you'd be so much further along by now.

Let all that go and begin right where you *are*.

Embrace practicing. (I'm *still* practicing!) Love your practice of offering coaching, making proposals and creating clients. And when someone tells you "no" or "I'll have to think about it," love that, too. Learn from all of it. Not everyone is going to hire you, but that doesn't matter. If you keep practicing, you'll have more than enough people wanting to work with you.

Let service become your personal alchemy,

Living Service ♥ 191

transmuting you in subtle yet significant ways. Embracing the attitude of service will soften the sharp edges of fear and insecurity and awaken innate feelings of compassion for others and for self. You will feel more comfortable in your own skin as you lose interest in what others think of you and even in what *you* think of you.

Let it take all the time it needs. Allow your judgment, frustration, self-doubt and worry to yield space in your life for living service so you can rise in this profession and in your life.

There is no "right way" to serve. There's your way. And you'll know you've found it when you feel an expansive feeling, an open-heartedness, a bigger than me-ness.

Service isn't just something we do. Deep down, after our ego's objections to it drop away, we realize that it's who we *are*. It's our true nature—love, connection and peace. When we awaken to this we experience life at the level of inspiration, with fresh eyes and softer hearts, open minds and open arms.

That's living service.

Acknowledgments

My heartfelt gratitude and deep appreciation go out to these loving, remarkable and talented people who came into my life as I've traveled on this service path (and continue to do so). Clients, colleagues, family and friends. All of you have shined a light for me, illuminating this path and my life.

- Dara Lurie, my book coach, who stayed with me on this journey and really "got me." Who knew that my detour would bring you to me?! Please find Dara at www.darajoycelurie.com
- Maurice Bassett, for your powerful service throughout my ACS experience and as my publisher. Thank you for your support in bringing this book to life.
- Chris Nelson, the best damn editor ever. Thank you for your wordsmithing, attention to detail and spot-on gut checks.
- David Michael Moore, for bringing my stories to life with your first-rate, exceptional illustrations.
- Karen Taylor, I love you with all my heart and I'm incredibly grateful for the amazing synchronicity of our journeys.
- Sherry Welsh, for your friendship and laughter, and for MSS

- Karen Davis, your #truthbombs kept waking me up! And you deliver with them with zero fanfare, which makes them even more impactful.
- Kamin Samuel, for the laughter and the honesty and for being an extraordinary, working coach.
- Tina Quinn, for your unending enthusiasm and loving support. Thank you for your light.
- Gary Mahler, for the game, our service family and your BIG vision.
- Dave Schwendiman, for your contagious laughter, insane creativity and playful genius.
- Ankush Jain, for your gentle, loving, powerful presence and the impact you make everywhere.
- Arminda Lindsay, for your love, honesty and our transformative growth chats.
- Therese Krieger, for our enduring, beautiful friendship and your laugh!
- Who the F#&K Do We Think We Are!!? Mastermind Group: Nadja Taranczewski, Vanessa Horn, Christine Livingston and Ginny Baillie, Thank you!
- Steve Parker, for the beginning and pointing me to the coaching world.
- My clients, for your commitment, courage and H.O.W. And for playing full out!
- All the coaches on the service path (past, present and future) who continue to inspire excellence.

- Mom & Dad, for your endless love, support and always wanting the best for me.
- Max and Elise, both of you are such a gift to me. I love you!
- Brian, for everything (including your fontology).

For the service path . . . that powerful antidote that saved me.

About the Author

Melissa Ford is a master business and life coach with over twenty years of experience working with individuals and groups. Her clients include fast-rising coaches, entrepreneurs, executives and career changers. She offers ongoing programs to coaches to help them strengthen their business mindsets, deepen their service and increase their profitability. She is a contributing author to *When All Boats Rise: 12 Coaches on Service as the Heart of a Thriving Practice.*

Visit Melissa at:

www.melissafordcoaching.com

Publisher's Catalogue

The Prosperous Series

#1 The Prosperous Coach: Increase Income and Impact for You and Your Clients (Steve Chandler and Rich Litvin)

#2 The Prosperous Hip Hop Producer: My Beat-Making Journey from My Grandma's Patio to a Six-Figure Business (Curtiss King)

* * *

Devon Bandison

Fatherhood Is Leadership: Your Playbook for Success, Self-Leadership, and a Richer Life

Sir Fairfax L. Cartwright

The Mystic Rose from the Garden of the King

Steve Chandler

37 Ways to BOOST Your Coaching Practice: PLUS: the 17 Lies That Hold Coaches Back and the Truth That Sets Them Free

50 Ways to Create Great Relationships

Business Coaching (Steve Chandler and Sam Beckford)

Crazy Good: A Book of CHOICES

CREATOR

Death Wish: The Path through Addiction to a Glorious Life

Fearless: Creating the Courage to Change the Things You Can

How to Get Clients

RIGHT NOW: Mastering the Beauty of the Present Moment

The Prosperous Coach: Increase Income and Impact for You and Your Clients (The Prosperous Series #1) (Steve Chandler and Rich Litvin)

Shift Your Mind Shift The World (Revised Edition)

Time Warrior: How to defeat procrastination, people-pleasing, self-doubt, over-commitment, broken promises and chaos

Wealth Warrior: The Personal Prosperity Revolution

Kazimierz Dąbrowski

Positive Disintegration

Charles Dickens

A Christmas Carol: A Special Full-Color, Fully-Illustrated Edition

Melissa Ford

Living Service: The Journey of a Prosperous Coach

James F. Gesualdi

Excellence Beyond Compliance: Enhancing Animal Welfare Through the Constructive Use of the Animal Welfare Act

Janice Goldman

Let's Talk About Money: The Girlfriends' Guide to Protecting Her ASSets

Sylvia Hall

This Is Real Life: Love Notes to Wake You Up

Christy Harden

Guided by Your Own Stars: Connect with the Inner Voice and Discover Your Dreams

I Heart Raw: Reconnection and Rejuvenation Through the Transformative Power of Raw Foods

Curtiss King

The Prosperous Hip Hop Producer: My Beat-Making Journey from My Grandma's Patio to a Six-Figure Business (The Prosperous Series #2)

David Lindsay

A Blade for Sale: The Adventures of Monsieur de Mailly

Abraham H. Maslow

The Aims of Education (audio)

The B-language Workshop (audio)

Being Abraham Maslow (DVD)

The Eupsychian Ethic (audio)

The Farther Reaches of Human Nature (audio)

Maslow and Self-Actualization (DVD)

Maslow on Management (audiobook)

Personality and Growth: A Humanistic Psychologist in the Classroom

Psychology and Religious Awareness (audio)

The Psychology of Science: A Reconnaissance

Self-Actualization (audio)

Weekend with Maslow (audio)

Albert Schweitzer

Reverence for Life: The Words of Albert Schweitzer

William Tillier

Personality Development Through Positive Disintegration: The Work of Kazimierz Dąbrowski

Margery Williams

The Velveteen Rabbit: or How Toys Become Real

Join our Mailing List:
www.MauriceBassett.com

MAURICE BASSETT
books for athletes of the mind

www.ingramcontent.com/pod-product-compliance
Lightning Source LLC
Chambersburg PA
CBHW071621170426
43195CB00038B/1675